Enterprise Risk Management

Enterprise Risk Management

A Methodology for Achieving Strategic Objectives

GREGORY MONAHAN

WILEY

John Wiley & Sons, Inc.

Published by John Wiley & Sons, Inc., Hoboken, New Jersey.

Published simultaneously in Canada.

For general information on our other products and services, or technical support, please contact our Customer Care Department within the United States at 800–762–2974, outside the United States at 317–572–3993, or fax 317–572–4002.

Wiley also publishes its books in a variety of electronic formats. Some content that appears in print may not be available in electronic books.

For more information about Wiley products, visit our Web site at http://www.wiley.com.

Library of Congress Cataloging-in-Publication Data

Monahan, Gregory, 1971-
  Enterprise risk management : a methodology for achieving strategic objectives/Gregory Monahan.
      p. cm. – (Wiley & SAS business series)
  Includes bibliographical references and index.
  ISBN 978-0-470-37233-3 (cloth)   1. Risk management.
  2. Decision making–Methodology.   3. Risk management–Methodology.   I. Title.
  HD61.M58 2008
  658.15'5–dc22

                                                                              2008023260

Printed in the United States of America

10   9   8   7   6   5   4   3   2   1

Wiley & SAS Business Series

The Wiley & SAS Business Series presents books that help senior-level managers with their critical management decisions.

Titles in the Wiley and SAS Business Series include:

Business Intelligence Competency Centers: A Team Approach to Maximizing Competitive Advantage, by Gloria J. Miller, Dagmar Brautigam, and Stefanie Gerlach

Case Studies in Performance Management: A Guide from the Experts, by Tony C. Adkins

CIO Best Practices: Enabling Strategic Value with Information Technology, by Joe Stenzel

Credit Risk Scorecards: Developing and Implementing Intelligent Credit Scoring, by Naeem Siddiqi

Customer Data Integration: Reaching a Single Version of the Truth, by Jill Dyche and Evan Levy

Fair Lending Compliance: Intelligence and Implications for Credit Risk Management, by Clark R. Abrahams and Mingyuan Zhang

Information Revolution: Using the Information Evolution Model to Grow Your Business, by Jim Davis, Gloria J. Miller, and Allan Russell

Marketing Automation: Practical Steps to More Effective Direct Marketing, by Jeff LeSueur

Performance Management: Finding the Missing Pieces (to Close the Intelligence Gap), by Gary Cokins

For more information on any of the above titles, please visit **www .wiley.com**.

I dedicate this book to those who made
My Big Fat Greek Wedding *such a wonderful experience.*

Contents

Preface

In recent years I have been amazed by the number of books written on the subject of risk management that completely fail to prescribe risk *measurement* techniques. If you are looking for a history of risk management or information on trends in risk management or case studies on best practices in risk management or insight on how to build the right (i.e., risk-sensitive) culture, then you need to refer to one of those other books. This book will do little for you if you are looking to build a business case for establishing the enterprise risk management office or obtain budget for resources to support your enterprise risk management framework. This book prescribes a process for the measurement of risk associated with the achievement of strategic objectives. Beyond prescribing measurement techniques, this book covers *some* of the aspects of managing risk. You might find that strange for a book about enterprise risk management; why would I deliberately exclude some elements of the "management" bit? I offer no excuse for this, just this explanation: There are elements to managing risk that are common to managing anything, and covering them here would be a complete waste of your time because I do not know these elements as well as the experts. I am sticking to what I know and what you cannot find elsewhere. I will cover those elements of management that need to be covered (i.e., those that relate directly to the effective use of the results of risk measurement). You can think of this book under an alternate title if you like: "Enterprise Risk Measurement and Its Application." I chose not to use that name purely for marketing reasons. My publisher recommended I call the book *Enterprise Risk Management: A Methodology for Achieving Strategic Objectives*, because "Enterprise Risk Management" and "Strategic Objectives" are very popular phrases. I like the title Wiley recommended because it reflects a core concept of my work, and that is to think of enterprise risk management as a means to achieving your strategic objectives.

Within this book I detail a methodology that will increase your chances of obtaining your strategic objectives. If reaching your strategic objectives is important to you, read on. The set of possible outcomes that may occur when you set off to achieve a strategic objective may be few or many in number. Regardless of how many there are, the outcomes can be classified into two groups: those that represent successful achievement of your objective or those that represent failure. In my experience, very few people responsible for the management of strategic plans (i.e., the plans conceived and then executed in order to reach strategic objectives) recognize the existence of this distribution. This is why so many plans result in failure (to meet the strategic objective). The methodology detailed in this book recognizes the entire distribution of possible outcomes but focuses on that part (or those parts) of the distribution that represents failure to achieve the objective.

While conducting research for this book, I had in mind the title "A Recipe for Enterprise Risk Management." I came across this statement in *Making Enterprise Risk Management Pay Off*, by T. L. Barton, W. G. Shenkir, and P. L. Walker:

> A cookbook recipe for implementing enterprise-wide risk management is not feasible because so much depends on the culture of the company and the change agents who lead the effort.

I thought that statement ridiculous, in particular because I believe that the implementation of anything of significant scope, such as enterprise risk management, should indeed be by the execution of predefined steps or the adherence to a recipe. The recipe is often referred to as the project plan, and it specifies, among other things, the tasks to be completed, the target completion dates, and the resources required. Perhaps Barton et al. used the word "implementing" incorrectly; maybe they meant "designing." I believe what they were trying to say was that they felt that the implementation of enterprise risk management had to be performed in a manner that was sensitive to the prevailing culture of the organization and that you would unlikely be able to follow someone else's approach. I must disagree. Despite what management consulting firms are likely to say on the subject of enterprise risk management, I am certain that the methodology published here can be implemented very easily. This book provides a recipe for enterprise risk management, and you do not have to boast three hats to follow it. The use of the word "recipe" requires, I feel, just a little more attention. For people who cannot cook, a recipe provides a means to produce an edible meal. For people who can cook, a recipe is usually the basis on which some experimentation might take place. I think the same is true of a project plan. For someone who has not done it before, the smart thing to do is follow the plan. If you have done it before, you might be qualified to add a pinch of salt here and there.

If you are unsure whether you need to apply enterprise risk management, this book offers little guidance beyond helping you understand the value of considering the distribution of possible outcomes associated with strategic objectives. I am not trying to promote the virtues of enterprise risk management; rather I am publishing a methodology for practitioners in this field. This book is written specifically for people who have recognized the value to their organization of (more effective) enterprise risk management and are struggling to determine what an *effective* enterprise risk management framework looks and feels like. The book can be used by a second audience, namely those people who are looking to invest in organizations and want either to apply the process prescribed here as part of their investment analysis or to judge the enterprise risk management framework of the potential investment with reference to the benchmark framework detailed here.

As I wrote this book, I sometimes considered an organization to be like an athlete. An athlete may begin an event with one or more of these aims: win, beat his or her personal best, or break a world record. Prior to the event, the athlete trains in a fashion that he or she believes returns the greatest chance of achieving the aim(s). The athlete's attitude is like the culture of the organization; belief in the objective(s) and the methods being employed to achieve it (them) is vital. Immediately prior to the event, the athlete has a predefined plan: go out hard, hang in the middle of the pack until midway, or something else. As the event unfolds, the athlete reviews his or her position, reconsiders the plan, and determines whether an adjustment is required. He or she also vigilantly checks the resources available and the environment in which he or she is acting. When the event is over, the aim(s) either have been met or not, and the athlete will feel a correlated level of (dis)satisfaction. Similarly, an organization begins with some desired outcomes in mind and with plans in place to achieve those outcomes. Usually those plans are reviewed in light of events, (changing) circumstances, and progressive measurement of achievement. At some time the organization will look back and say "Well, we aimed to do X and we achieved Y." Just like the athlete, the members of the organization will (or should) feel some level of (dis)satisfaction.

Finally, this book is not designed to help you determine organizational strategy or, otherwise stated, set strategic objectives. The methodology introduced here is about managing the risks associated with strategic objectives and strategic plans. It can be applied once the strategic objectives have been defined. Having said that, application of the methodology to defined objectives may lead to a review of those objectives, as application of the methodology may lead owners of the strategic plans to conclude that the risks associated with the objectives are unacceptable. As a brief aside, I often wonder how organizations determine their strategic objectives. When reviewing strategic objectives, it is quite interesting to ask "Why?" For example, someone might say "Our objective is to be number one in customer service." When someone says that to you, reply, "Oh," then pause and ask: "Why?" and see what they say. The methodology prescribed here does not discriminate between meaningful and not-so-meaningful objectives.

Acknowledgments

I would like to thank two distinct groups of people for providing me the motivation to write this book. The first group comprises those people who make life more complex than it needs to be and hide behind molehills as if they are mountains. Well, I can see you, so there is no mountain between us. The frustration you have caused me throughout my working life is my major source of motivation for this book. The second, much smaller, group includes those people who have demonstrated the ability and confidence to sort things out. These people are forever questioning the status quo and approach existing benchmarks with disdain. This book is for both groups of people. If you are in the first group, this book provides a step-by-step guide to reaching the summit of your enterprise risk management mountain. When you finish this book, you will have no excuse not to implement an effective enterprise risk management framework. For the second group, this book sets a new benchmark, and I am more than happy for you to approach it with the disdain that drives you. I am equally happy for you to take the benchmark set here and attempt to raise it; in fact, I challenge you to do so, believing that only good can come of your attempts. I hope you succeed and write about it.

Throughout my career in risk management and related areas, such as risk management systems, I have been privileged to know and work with some very bright and enthusiastic individuals, but I am not going to mention any of them here. The reason for not mentioning particular individuals is because I cannot really identify the contribution each has made to my own understanding of or interest in the field. By posing some question in passing, such as "If I have a set of 10,000 unique numbers and I randomly draw 1,000 subsets of 250 numbers, what is the probability that I will get at least two sets that are the same?" or by making some comment during casual conversation, like "We are due for another massive corporate failure," you have, perhaps inadvertently, fueled my fire. Thank you.

Introduction

This book introduces a methodology for the management of risks faced by organizations: strategic objectives at risk (SOAR). It employs a process with "SOAR" as its acronym. I differentiate between a methodology and a process in this way: A process is a series of predefined steps that, when executed, results in some outcome(s). A methodology is a framework that encompasses a number of elements, including, in particular, people and processes. This book focuses on the application of the SOAR process to risks associated with strategic objectives. I believe risk management has been inadequately applied to this field to date, largely because no one has been able to define a widely acceptable methodology. The SOAR methodology is not restricted to this application; in fact, it can be applied to managing any desired (and uncertain) outcome.

One of the titles I considered for this book was "A Recipe for Enterprise Risk Management." If you think of a recipe as "a formula or procedure for doing or attaining something," as it is described in Webster's dictionary, then this is precisely what this book provides. This definition implies that if you want to get the result, you have to actually do something. This book simply tells you what it is you need to do. Another familiar definition of "recipe" is "a set of instructions for making something from various ingredients." The first part of this definition is practically the same as that given in Webster's dictionary, but the second part adds something new: the concept of ingredients. This book identifies the ingredients required to conduct effective enterprise risk management.

Enterprise risk management should not be confused with other similar concepts, such as enterprise-wide risk management. Within this book I prescribe a methodology for managing risks associated with strategic objectives. Literature abounds on how to manage other risk types, such as market risk, reputational risk, operational risk, project risk, or credit risk. Enterprise-wide risk management is (usually) about ensuring that the organization has in place risk management frameworks for each of these different risk types and does not attempt to address risk management in terms of the overall health of the organization as it strives to achieve its stated objectives. Enterprise-wide risk management (usually) relates to the notion of providing senior managers a one-stop shop (often represented by the popularly named "dashboard") where they can check that each of the business units is managing the risks it faces. The process usually involves the collection of megabytes of data from every nook and cranny of every office around the globe, the collation of data and storage in an "enterprise data warehouse," and the production of many (usually *too* many) reports, including OLAP (online analytical processing). You have *got* to have OLAP reports, right? I am a firm believer in the notion that data is king, but I believe there are two different types of data: useful data and rubbish. The SOAR methodology relies on data. The timely collection, collation, analysis, and dissemination of data is critical to successful execution of the SOAR process. Nonetheless, the volume of data required under the SOAR process is likely to be tiny. The two most important characteristics of data employed within the SOAR process are that it be accurate and timely; quality is certainly more important than quantity.

I advocate that the enterprise risk management framework be managed by an independent enterprise risk management office, that is, a dedicated group of resources who are completely independent of any of the operational units within the organization. I believe that the enterprise risk management office has the greatest chance of success if it is operationally independent of the organization, subject to appropriate transparency of the organization. I object to ownership of the enterprise risk management program by the chief financial officer or internal audit for a number of reasons, discussed in detail later. I will say just a few words now. The SOAR methodology is not an audit process; it is a management process. I advocate that the process be controlled by a dedicated enterprise risk management office for a few reasons. The first one is to make enterprise risk management *seem* important. Because of the long-term nature of strategic objectives and because the activities associated with strategic plans often are quite removed from daily operations, you can imagine that a process around managing risks associated with strategic objectives might be considered unnecessary. Skeptics might argue that organizations have been achieving strategic objectives so far and suggest that a disciplined approach to the management of risk is not required. As mentioned earlier, I am not going to sell the concept of enterprise risk management. The results of enterprise risk management under the SOAR methodology will speak for themselves in time. I am certain that organizations managing their strategic plans under the SOAR methodology will be more successful than those that manage their strategic objectives by any other method, including no method. Until then, I believe it is a good idea to help people believe in both the concept and the methodology by making it seem important through the dedication of expert resources. The second reason for an independent enterprise risk management function is to test the importance of your strategic objective. If it is not important enough to warrant investment in dedicated resources, why are you doing it? The third reason for recommending that the SOAR methodology be owned and managed by a dedicated enterprise risk management office is to ensure it is applied correctly. In time, senior managers responsible for the management of strategic objectives may be qualified in the SOAR methodology, just as some people are Six Sigma black belts. At that time, a dedicated enterprise risk management office may not be essential, and responsibility for management of the SOAR methodology can be given to the owner of the objective.

I need to note a couple of things on the example (strategic) objectives I use throughout this book. In stating the example objectives, I have been lazy. I might, for example, say something like "The objective is to increase profit." I know that this is a poorly defined objective; a better expression of that objective might be something like "The objective is to increase group net profit by 10% per annum over the next three years." I am a big fan of SMART (specific, measurable, actionable, realistic, time-bound) objectives, but I am also an advocate of focus. The focus of this book is not on defining (strategic) objectives, so I have deliberately belittled the objective through lazy expression of it. This book demands that you consider strategic objectives as desired outcomes for which you are striving and that you recognize that the desired outcome is one of many possible outcomes. Just think of playing Frisbee with someone. Ordinarily, you attempt to throw the Frisbee so the person can (run a bit and) catch it. If the person misses it and it hits them in the eye, blinding him or her permanently, you have failed to achieve your objective despite correctly executing your plan. The point is that execution of almost any plan has multiple possible outcomes (usually of varying probabilities), some of which are more desirable than others. If you think of a plan that has only one certain outcome, good for you. That sort of outcome (and its associated plan) does not need management of the type prescribed here.

A fundamental prerequisite for applying the SOAR methodology is that a number of outcomes are possible and that they are not all equally desirable. If all of the possible outcomes are equally satisfactory (in relation to achieving your objective), then risk management is not required. Furthermore, you should apply (risk) management only if you have the ability to influence the outcome. Let us say you hold a traditional six-sided die and you want to roll a 1; that is, rolling a 1 is your (most highly) desired outcome. You know you have a 1 in 6 chance, right? Unless you have the ability to manipulate the die itself, by, say, replacing the 2 with a 1, or weighting the 6, you should just throw it and cross your fingers for luck.

I would like to examine one of the prerequisite conditions—that the outcomes are not equally desirable—in a little more detail. I will do so without going too deeply into a fascinating and equally frustrating field that I am determined to avoid: human behavior. Not highlighting the fact that human behavior undermines the robustness of the SOAR methodology (and any other methodology that requires human intervention) could be considered negligent. Or I could excuse my failure to mention it on the basis that I assumed everyone knows that humans are irrational and there is no reason for this to change simply because the SOAR methodology is applied. Here I will talk about human behavior as it relates to desire. I will talk about one other area of human behavior—risk aversion or risk appetite—a little later as part of our discussion on managing human behavior, one of the elements of the "react" step of the SOAR process.

In the 1700s, Daniel Bernoulli posed the notions of expected utility and diminishing marginal utility. Expressed very simply, Bernoulli suggested that the same outcome does not produce the same effect on different people. An example might be the "value" person A derives from winning $100 versus the "value" person B gets from winning $100. Bernoulli suggests that if person A is wealthier than person B, person A will derive less "value" from the prize. Sounds reasonable to me. I have written "value" in quotation marks as it is a somewhat tricky term to define. Alternatives might be joy, pleasure, satisfaction, or even utility (to name a few). Whether you accept the detail of the theory (you may find it interesting to read) or not, Bernoulli's theory has implications for the application of the SOAR methodology. Furthermore, Bernoulli suggested that the same outcome may not always be judged to provide the same value by the same person under different circumstances. An example of this might be a person's decision to travel X miles to save $5 off a $10 item but decide not to travel the same distance to save the same amount off a $1,000 item.

The SOAR methodology aims to steer the organization toward attaining its strategic objectives. As soon as you recognize a strategic objective as a "desired outcome," the implication of Bernoulli's theory slaps you in the face; "desire" (differing from pleasure only in time) is a personal thing and tricky to measure. So how can the desirability of different outcomes be measured accurately? Even when the possible outcomes are unambiguously measurable, their desirability is not. The example just given is a great example; a saving of $5 is worth exactly $5, regardless of the original value of an item, but Bernoulli's theory suggests that the "value" to the saver is not consistent. Take the case where an organization wishes to achieve sales of $100 million over the next 12 months. Will achieving sales of $95 million be completely unacceptable, or is it almost as good (say 95% as good) as hitting the target? What if the organization achieves sales of $105 million; is that better, worse, or the same as achieving the desired level? When money is involved, it is usually pretty reasonable to take the monetary value as a proxy for "value" (or the measure of desire), but more is not always better, as the excess can be used as evidence of a lack of control over outcomes. One example of this is where an organization reports greater than forecast profit and its stock price falls!

This book prescribes a methodology that enables you to increase the chances of attaining your organizational objectives. The methodology includes rules for determining metrics to measure outcomes. Acknowledging the merit in Bernoulli's utility theory, the method requires that metrics incorporate desirability. A quick example might be in relation to a financial objective: to achieve sales of 100 million units over the next year. We could set the metric as "number of units sold" and we could set the target value equal to 100. Or we could get a little more sophisticated and do something like set the metric equal to "sales objective metric" (something that we just made up) and set the target value equal to 3. If the number of units sold is between 95 and 110, then sales objective metric equals 3. If the number of units sold is between 90 and 95, then the metric value equals 2; and for sales less than 90, the metric equals 1. If the number of units sold is anything above 110, the metric value is 2. The reasons for taking this approach include our need to include the notion of "desirability" in the measurement of the outcome. If sales of 100 million units and 101 million units are equally desirable, we may as well treat those two possible outcomes as equally desirable. You do not have to do it this way. We will discuss the process for setting metric values in detail later as part of the set step of the SOAR process. For now, just keep in mind that we have discussed the notion of "desirability" and I have suggested that our measurement should include this concept.

Enterprise Risk
Management

CHAPTER 1

Defining Enterprise Risk Management

A trusted colleague and friend advised me that I should not begin with a definition of the term "enterprise risk management." After much deliberation, I have decided to include my definition, because I feel it is imperative that you and I share a common understanding of what I am writing about in this book. If you accept my definition, then you can consider everything else I espouse within the context of this definition. If you prefer some other definition, you probably should consider whether the other things I say need to be adjusted for your preferred definition. That said, and with respect and thanks to my friend for his advice, I begin with definitions gleaned from *Merriam-Webster's Eleventh Collegiate Dictionary* of each of the words in the phrase:

Enterprise A unit of economic organization or activity; especially: a business organization

Let us proceed on the basis that an enterprise is a group of legal vehicles, divisions, business units, and so forth that make up an organization. I like the term "organization," because it seems to carry less connotation about the nature of the organization than, say, "company" or "business." In my view, "organization" carries no connotation of size, operation, or objective; it could just as easily be a local symphony orchestra as it could be the U.S. Federal Reserve or Barclays PLC. So an "enterprise" is an organization.

Risk Someone or something that creates or suggests a hazard

Here we need to move away from the dictionary definition (with all due respect) and consider a more professional, as opposed to casual, definition. What we are really talking about is variability; that is, risk is anything that produces a distribution of various outcomes of various probabilities. From here on think of "risk" as meaning "uncertainty," and imagine that we can represent that uncertainty as a distribution of possible outcomes of varying probabilities. I know we cannot always do that with a great deal of certainty or ease, and I am not suggesting we need to be able to. I am hoping that each time you read the word "risk" you will visualize a distribution of outcomes and associated probabilities. It might look like a typical normal (bell-shaped) distribution, or it might not; it does not matter.

In addition to defining risk, we need to consider those things that go hand in hand with risk. The SOAR (Strategic Objectives At Risk) methodology views risk in this context: Risk thrives on risk drivers or causes and manifests itself in events that have consequences (or outcomes). Let me repeat as this is an absolutely vital element to our definition of risk: Risk manifests itself in events that have consequences. Once you recognize that you are faced with a particular risk, you have to accept the fact that an event can happen and that it will have consequences. The SOAR methodology defines a process that (1) enables you to determine whether to take the risk and (2) prepares you for the consequence of an event. The other element in the risk universe is risk mitigation, or controls. The risk universe can be viewed in Exhibit 1.1.

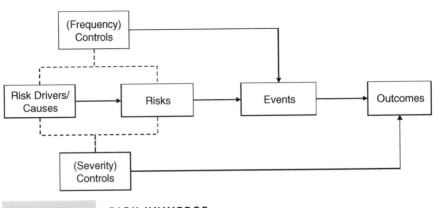

EXHIBIT 1.1   **RISK UNIVERSE**

In the exhibit, you can see what you often hear—for example, you might hear someone talk about:

- The risk of being hit by a car (being hit by a car is an event.)
- The risk of serious injury (serious injury is an outcome.)

From an organizational point of view:

- In key man risk, the event is someone of perceived importance leaving.
- In the risk associated with entering new markets, an event might be failure to adhere to local regulations.

I do not want to focus on the definition of risk, but I feel it necessary to comment on the definition of "risk" offered by Deloitte in "The Risk Intelligent Enterprise":

> Risk is the potential for loss caused by an event (or series of events) that can adversely affect the achievement of a company's objectives.[1]

Despite the fact that the definition recognizes only losses and adverse effects, Deloitte then goes on to say:

> The Risk Intelligent Enterprise views risk not just as vulnerability to the downside, but also preparedness for the upside.

I ask you this: Why would anyone who accepts the Deloitte definition of "risk" be prepared for upside? Consider also this definition: "The key is not to predict the future, but to be prepared for it."[2] The author, Pericles, fails to address the obvious question: "Prepare for what?"

It is sometimes difficult to articulate certain risks. The best way to get around this problem is to use the type of language employed in the examples given earlier. Let us say you are building a tunnel for a road under an existing structure (e.g., a city), and someone asks you to identify the risks you face. Do you say something like "tunneling risk"? Or "inaccurate measurement risk"? These are not very helpful responses. A more meaningful answer might be something like: "We might do something wrong that causes the tunnel to collapse and the stuff on top falls in, destroying buildings and killing people." Without really giving any definition of or name to the "risk," you have clearly articulated a driver (do something wrong), a possible event (collapse of the tunnel), and a couple of outcomes:

Buildings collapse and people die. The truth is, it does not really matter what you call the risk, or even whether you can clearly articulate it. However, it is absolutely essential that you are able very clearly to define those things around the risk: the drivers, the controls, the possible events, and the possible outcomes.

Let us work backward through the risk paradigm starting with one of our strategic objectives as the desired outcome. In this case, the outcome we seek (or objective we aim to achieve) is to be recognized as the country's best employer. Let us imagine that our distribution of possible outcomes includes us being rated as the worst, the best, or something in between. For ease, we will limit the outcomes to best, good, middle of the pack, poor, and worst. Our role, as enterprise risk management officers, is to manage a process that will provide the people responsible for the outcome(s) the best chance of achieving their desired outcome(s). The focus of that process must be on those elements that can influence the outcomes. From Exhibit 1.1, we can see that the elements that influence outcomes are (working backward from right to left):

- Events
- Risks
- Risk drivers
- Controls

Risks

I have defined "risk" as meaning "uncertainty," and I have proposed that the presence of risk (uncertainty) is evident in the distribution of possible outcomes. I think it is easy to fall into the trap of spending way too long trying to determine a clear definition of each risk associated with an objective. Take, for example, the case where your objective is to increase total revenues by at least 10% over the next year. You could, quite simply, summarize all of the risks you face as "the probability that we do not increase total revenues by 10% over the next year." Is that sufficient for application of the SOAR process? Absolutely.

In truth, I have included "risks" in my view of the risk universe only because I thought everyone would expect to see it there and that great numbers of readers would rebel if I did not include it. For the application of the SOAR process, I advocate that risks be stated as in the previous example (i.e., the one about increasing total revenues), for three reasons:

1. By simply defining risk as the probability of not obtaining your objective, you maintain your focus on the fundamental concept of the SOAR methodology: You face a distribution of possible outcomes of varying reward and probability.

2. You do not waste time debating possible (and completely academic) definitions of the risks you face.

3. You have a much higher likelihood of identifying all of the possible influential factors—namely drivers and controls—and this is where your focus should be.

Risk Drivers

Risk drivers and controls are factors that influence the outcome. I distinguish between them as follows: Risk drivers are factors that increase uncertainty while controls are factors that are intended to reduce uncertainty or help soften the blow of an adverse outcome. It is useful to think of drivers and controls in terms of their impact on the distribution of possible outcomes. Take the case where there are no risk drivers; that is, the outcome is certain. In this case, the (certain) outcome could be represented as a single value on a graph (see Exhibit 1.2).

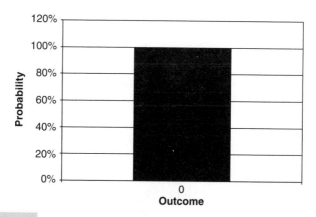

EXHIBIT 1.2   CERTAIN OUTCOME

In the presence of risk drivers, the distribution of possible outcomes might look something like Exhibit 1.3.

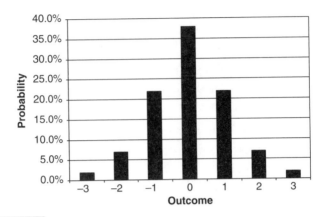

EXHIBIT I.3   SIMPLE DISTRIBUTION OF OUTCOMES

Without any form of analysis whatsoever, let us assume that the greater the number of risk drivers, the greater the number of possible outcomes and that increasing the number of risk drivers flattens and broadens the distribution. This (assumed) effect can be seen in Exhibit 1.4.

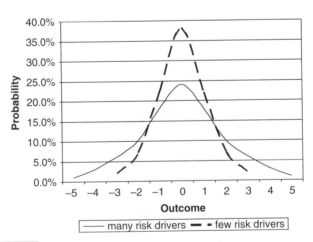

EXHIBIT I.4   DISTRIBUTIONS OF OUTCOMES INFLUENCED BY A DIFFERENT NUMBER OF RISK DRIVERS

The fact is, of course, that our assumption is not always true. It will not always be the case that more risk drivers leads to a flattening and broadening of the distribution of possible outcomes. Furthermore, a single driver of risk A may produce a different distribution of possible outcomes than a single driver of risk B; the driver of risk A may produce something like the tall, thin distribution in Exhibit 1.4 while the driver of risk B may produce the shorter, wider distribution. Which would you rather face?

Controls

As discussed earlier, risk drivers and controls are factors that influence the outcome. I stated that controls are intended to reduce uncertainty or soften the blow. The term "intended" is used for a reason—to highlight the fact that controls are created with thought, as opposed to drivers, which simply exist. In addition, the term "intended" implies that the reality may differ from the idea; that is a control may not have the intended effect.

Similar to the difference between distributions of outcomes influenced by few risk drivers and those influenced by many risk drivers, distributions influenced by controls should be taller and narrower than distributions not influenced by controls. That is really the primary responsibility of the enterprise risk management office—to raise and narrow the distribution (of possible outcomes) around the desired outcome. The identification and application of controls is the most critical element of the SOAR process and the main reason for the enterprise risk management office to exist. Controls do not always soften the blow; often they are designed to avoid the hit altogether. In language more suitable to the context, controls are measures that are put in place to reduce the probability or severity of an adverse outcome. It is unusual for a control to be designed to reduce both frequency and severity. The brakes on a car are a good example of a control that reduces both frequency and severity. If you did not have brakes, you can be pretty sure you would crash more frequently than if you did have brakes. If you had an accident without braking, you can be pretty sure the damage would be worse than if you had braked. An airbag, however, can reduce the severity, but it is not intended to address the likelihood of an accident. A quick word of caution on the use of controls: Be careful they do not incite recklessness. To continue the car theme a moment, have you ever been in a car when the driver has said something like "strap in" as he accelerates? The implication is that the driver thinks he can take more risk if the control is in place. In the context of application of the SOAR process, there is probably little to worry about—just keep in mind that the application of controls *may* influence behaviors in a way that you did not intend.

Inherent and Residual Risk

Exhibit 1.5 introduces the concepts of inherent and residual risk. Inherent risk is the raw or untreated risk that produces the set of possible outcomes, without controls. Controls are the vehicles employed by the enterprise risk management office to mitigate inherent risk and I, like many others, refer to mitigated risk as "residual risk." In the absence of controls, residual risk equals inherent risk. More generally, we can express the relationship as:

Residual risk = inherent risk − impact of controls

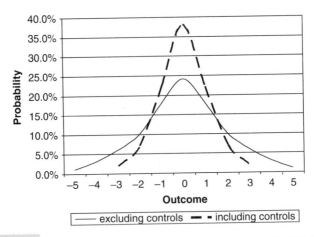

EXHIBIT I.5   **DISTRIBUTIONS OF OUTCOMES INCLUDING AND EXCLUDING THE INFLUENCE OF CONTROLS (INHERENT AND RESIDUAL RISK)**

The equation is not strictly correct mathematically, as we have defined risk as being represented by a distribution, and the distributions of inherent risk and the impact of controls are not directly additive. However, the equation is good enough for our purpose, which is to show that controls are the tools we use to reduce risk.

Residual risk should be the main focus of the enterprise risk manager as residual risk drives the distribution of possible outcomes and it is the distribution of possible outcomes that we are aiming to understand and manage. An understanding of residual risk implies an understanding of inherent risk, though that may not always be the case. If, for example, some unidentified control exists, it would be possible to mistake residual risk for inherent risk. An example would be something like active suspension in a car that stiffens to prevent body roll when cornering. As the driver, you may not know that the technology (i.e., the control) prevented you from having an accident (i.e., an event) as you took a corner at 80 miles an hour.

Events

Events are things that happen. They are important to the enterprise risk management office (and the SOAR process) for four reasons:

1. They evidence the presence of risk.
2. We can learn from them.
3. They have consequences, and these consequences are the things that we are trying to achieve or avoid.
4. They precede an outcome, so we may still have the ability to influence the outcome.

Outcomes

Outcomes are the consequences of events. Despite the fact that they are the ultimate element in the flow of risk, they can be controlled (i.e., they can be subject to the impact of controls). Consider, for example, the very common case of a car accident. The accident is an event. The outcome could be that your car is written off and you have to buy a new one, at a replacement cost of $20,000. In the presence of insurance, the *financial* impact (or outcome) of the event might be reduced to just $500, representing the policy excess (or deductible amount). This is the type of thing to which I was referring earlier when I mentioned "softening the blow" as part of our discussion on risk drivers.

MANAGEMENT

There are a couple of appropriate definitions for management:

Management   Judicious use of means to accomplish an end
   and
   the conducting or supervising of something (as a business)

Think of "management" as meaning "dealing with it." But I must spend a moment on the meaning of "judicious" as it forms part of the definition of "management":

Judicious   Having, exercising, or characterized by sound judgment

Those of you who know me even just a little might be expecting me to make some crack about the contradiction between "management" and "sound judgment," but I'm not going to, because we are using the term "management" as it relates to action rather than as a body of people. What I really want to point out is that "management" involves the application of (sound) judgment. If judgment is involved, will that add to the uncertainty? Unfortunately, the answer is more likely to be yes than no. But fear not, we will "manage" that!

Without thinking too much, we can imagine that our ability to influence the outcome decreases as we approach the outcome or rather that we have the greatest ability to influence the outcome if we can manipulate the risk drivers (causes) and the controls. Back to our example of aiming to be recognized as the country's best employer. Let us say employers are assessed on an annual basis, and the assessment is based on the results of surveys of employees. In order to be rated "best employer," we must get the highest average score across surveyed employees of a number of employers. We want our employees to recognize things we do as being in line with the actions of a great employer. In other words, we want to produce a number of outcomes that please our employees. Imagine that we decide to issue shares (i.e., the *event*) under a bonus scheme expecting that the *outcome* will be our employees think we are a great employer. With an enterprise risk management hat on, we consider the fact that our desired outcome is one of a range of possible outcomes, and we need to consider ways to maximize the probability of achieving our desired outcome. We recognize that one outcome that might eventuate is the bulk of employees become disgruntled at the inequity of the share allocation, which seems to favor employees who already receive higher salaries. Still wearing the enterprise risk management hat, we would also consider that being rated "best" is a relative assessment, and that means that we need to consider what other employers are doing too. From that broader point of view, the enterprise risk management office needs to recognize the assessment of the organization of which it is a part relative to other employers as the ultimate outcome—or, rather, distribution of outcomes. From this point of view, events that lead to favorable outcomes include things our organization does well and things other organizations do poorly. Say, for example, that we were ranked second in last year's survey. If nothing changed other than the company ranked number one dissolved, we would be number one.

The enterprise risk management office has to determine the universe of possible outcomes and their probabilities, then look back at how those events might unfold and what the organization could do to make sure the events unfold according to a plan that maximizes the chance of attaining the goal. In doing so, the enterprise risk management office may have to accept that some elements of the ultimate outcome are beyond its control—such as the actions of other organizations that thrill their employees. Given that these are beyond their control, should the enterprise risk management office ignore them? Absolutely not. The organization must recognize risks beyond its control; in the case of unmanageable risks, the function of the enterprise risk management office is to help prepare the organization for the possible outcomes, albeit in the knowledge that the organization is unable to influence the outcome. Adverse outcomes still can be managed. Say that, despite our best efforts, we end up ranked second . . . again! "Managing" the outcome might involve preparing a cleverly articulated press release expressing delight at maintaining the second position and praising the efforts of all involved for helping the organization achieve this enviable result.

ENTERPRISE RISK MANAGEMENT

What is our definition of enterprise risk management? Simple.

Enterprise Risk Management   Dealing with uncertainty for the organization

I do not want to make it any more complex than that; there is nothing to gain from doing so. I will, however, bound the application of the methodology presented within this book to uncertain outcomes that should be dealt with at an organizational level as opposed to, say, by a line manager. To this end, I advocate the application of this methodology to the strategic objectives of the organization. This restriction is not inherent within the methodology; if you wish, you can apply it more broadly. I apply the methodology at this level because I see the management of risks associated with strategic objectives as being the most poorly addressed problem facing organizations today. I have developed the methodology to address this problem: a failure to manage the risks associated with attempting to achieve strategic objectives. By both the title and content of this book, I propose that enterprise risk management is defined as a methodology for managing risks associated with strategic objectives of an organization.

▓ NOTES

1. Deloitte Touche Tohmatsu, "The Risk Intelligent Enterprise—ERM Done Right," Deloitte Development LLC, 2006.
2. Pericles, 495–429 BC.

CHAPTER 2

Strategic Objectives

Chapter 1 presented two different definitions of enterprise risk management. The colloquial one was "dealing with uncertainty for the organization" and the slightly more formal one was "(a) methodology for managing risks associated with strategic objectives of an organization." The more formal definition deliberately included the application to strategic objectives as I wanted to maintain a focus on the risks associated with strategic objectives, as opposed to the myriad risks faced by organizations on a daily basis. There is the risk that Jim from the warehouse does not show up today, but that is not what we want to be concerned with. The SOAR methodology detailed here can indeed be applied to manage that risk, but I suspect that would be an example of overkill. Rather, let us focus our attention on those items with an uncertain outcome where achievement of the *desired* outcome is fundamental to the health of the organization.

For convenience, strategic objectives are grouped into three categories: financial, market, and operational. The taxonomy is not really important. You can define any grouping you feel is appropriate for your organization, perhaps based on organizational structure or ownership of strategic objectives or anything else. What is important is coverage; your classification system must cover all of the strategic objectives to which you wish to apply the methodology. Once you understand the methodology, in particular the usage of metrics, you should see some sense in the categorization I provide. I have grouped the objectives that share common or like metrics. Having said that, once you understand the methodology, you may well derive a classification that differs to the one proposed here and makes more sense to your organization.

FINANCIAL OBJECTIVES

Of all of the risks facing an organization, those that impact bottom-line numbers are, for pretty obvious reasons, the most popular ones. By "popular" I mean they receive the most attention. There are a number of reasons for this, including the fact that data is usually publicly available (often by law), the subject is what drives the vast majority of organizations and their investors, and, to date, this data has been the easiest to obtain and understand. Although there are probably hundreds, possibly thousands, of variations, financial objectives typically boil down to two categories: strength of the balance sheet and financial performance.

Statement of Financial Position

The statement of financial position (formerly known as the balance sheet) records the organization's financial position at any point in time. It categorizes the organization's objects into things the organization owns (assets) and things the organization owes (liabilities and owners' equity). Some typical financial objectives that relate to the statement of financial position are listed in Exhibit 2.1.

EXHIBIT 2.1   STRATEGIC OBJECTIVE METRICS RELATING TO THE STATEMENT OF FINANCIAL POSITION

Objective	Metric[a]
Increase assets	Total assets
Reduce liabilities	Total liabilities
Return on assets	Profit/assets
Return on equity	Profit/equity
Asset turnover	Sales/assets
Financial leverage	Assets/equity
Debt to assets ratio	Liabilities/assets
Debt to equity ratio	Liabilities/equity
Current ratio	Current assets/current liabilities

[a]Categories for metrics are defined later. The metrics listed here would fall into the "metrics for strategic objectives" class.

Statement of Financial Performance

The statement of financial performance (formerly known as the profit and loss statement) shows how well the organization performed, at least with respect to those things measured by accountants over a certain period. Partly because of my background in risk management, I am not a huge fan of accounting, but as far as financial objectives go, I have to admit that you probably do not have to look much further than the financial statements to identify metrics for financial objectives. Exhibit 2.2 provides examples of objectives relating to the statement of financial performance.

EXHIBIT 2.2	STRATEGIC OBJECTIVE METRICS RELATING TO THE STATEMENT OF FINANCIAL PERFORMANCE

Objective	Metric
Total shareholder return	Growth in share value, assuming dividend reinvestment
Increase revenue	Revenue
Reduce costs	Expenses
Profit margin	Profit/sales
Payout ratio	Dividends/profit
Interest cover ratio	Earnings before interest and/tax interest expense
Earnings per share	Profit/shares issued
Price/earnings ratio	Share price/earnings per share
Dividend yield	Dividend per share/current share price

MARKET OBJECTIVES

The category of market objectives focuses on the position of the organization within its marketplace(s); that is, how it is placed (or perceived to be placed) relative to its competitors; with its suppliers, partners, and customers; and by its regulators. Take, for example, the case where a charitable organization sets as one of its objectives to become the most trusted charity by some certain date. That is an objective that positions the organization with or relative to its customers, its competitors, and its regulators.

Customers

Customers are the entities who "purchase" the products/services offered by the organization. I say "purchase" in an attempt to include all forms of transactions from, say, the purchase of a tollway by a consortium of investors, to a donation by an individual to World Vision. Exhibit 2.3 provides examples of objectives relating to customers.

EXHIBIT 2.3   STRATEGIC OBJECTIVE METRICS RELATING TO CUSTOMERS

Objective	Metric
Be rated number 1 in customer service	Customer service survey result
Increase market share	Firm's sales/total market sales
Increase share of wallet	Monetary value of spend with us/total spend
Increase profitability	Gross or net profit
Increase frequency of transaction	Time interval between transactions or number of transactions per time period
Increase average value of transaction	Average value of transaction
Broaden product portfolio	Average number of products sold per customer

Suppliers

Suppliers are organizations that provide inputs in some incomplete form; that is, they supply things that are further modified before final "sale" (sale is quoted for the same reason as "purchased") or they supply products/services that are required to sustain the operations of the organization—things like paper for the photocopy machine, the photocopy machine for . . . photocopies, chairs, desks, tanks . . . whatever. Exhibit 2.4 provides examples of objectives relating to suppliers.

EXHIBIT 2.4   STRATEGIC OBJECTIVE METRICS RELATING TO SUPPLIERS

Objective	Metric
Consolidate suppliers	Number of suppliers
Increase supply chain efficiency	Amount saved through revenue-sharing contracts
On-time delivery	Number of deliveries within n minutes of schedule
Order fill accuracy	Number of orders filled correctly

Competitors

I know; you do not have competitors, do you? Because you have something unique—or at least a unique selling *proposition*: your brand, or your great product, or the fact that you have twice as many outlets as that other organization. I have got to admit, I am quite skeptical of the old "unique selling proposition"—face it, the difference between uniqueness and being one of the pack is simply, and almost always, time. (A notable exception is when the uniqueness you offer is in the form of a human.) And you can pause or fast-forward time through the acquisition of (potential) competitors, right? Exhibit 2.5 provides examples of objectives relating to competitors.

EXHIBIT 2.5   STRATEGIC OBJECTIVE METRICS RELATING TO COMPETITORS

Objective	Metric
Be the lowest-cost producer	Cost of goods sold
Offer a substantially different product	Points of differentiation

Partners

Partners are your organization's dance partners: other organizations with which you cooperate to mutual advantage. You might be a software company and have a partner that develops hardware, or you might be a metal company and have a partner that develops a rust-resistant undercoat. Exhibit 2.6 provides examples of objectives relating to partners.

EXHIBIT 2.6   STRATEGIC OBJECTIVE METRICS RELATING TO PARTNERS

Objective	Metric
Build strategic partnerships	Monetary value of joint business with partner
Diversification	Value of business conducted with one partner as a percentage of business conducted with all partners

Regulators

Almost all organizations operate within regulated markets. Regulators are those organizations that believe that someone within the market will operate in a manner that unfairly disadvantages someone else, and so they regulate to try to prevent that. Exhibit 2.7 provides an example of an objective relating to regulators.

EXHIBIT 2.7   STRATEGIC OBJECTIVE METRIC RELATING TO REGULATORS

Objective	Metric
Make operations more transparent to regulator	Number of reports sent to regulator

OPERATIONAL OBJECTIVES

Within the category of operational objectives are the navel-gazing elements of the organization: the assessment of what happens internally and how it impacts (or adds risk to) the achievement of the strategic objectives. Here we look at the people, processes, and systems employed by the organization to make things happen.

Corporate Governance

You need not think too hard to recall one or two magnificent corporate disasters caused by a failure in some aspect of corporate governance, such as Enron and WorldCom. Exhibit 2.8 provides examples of objectives relating to corporate governance.

EXHIBIT 2.8   STRATEGIC OBJECTIVE METRICS RELATING TO CORPORATE GOVERNANCE

Objective	Metric
Publish accurate financial statements	Number of negative findings by auditors
Protect the organization against internal fraud	Dollar value of losses due to internal fraud

Human Resources

Organizations are synthetic legal vehicles without heart or soul. Nonetheless, they live and breathe via the (noses of the) people who work for them.

The "human resources" category involves objectives relating to your . . . human resources. Exhibit 2.9 provides examples of objectives relating to human resources.

EXHIBIT 2.9 **STRATEGIC OBJECTIVE METRICS RELATING TO HUMAN RESOURCES**

Objective	Metric
Increase employee satisfaction	Staff satisfaction survey result
Reduce staff turnover	Staff turnover

Management Team

This book is about managing risks associated with achievement of strategic objectives. I would be negligent if I did not identify the senior management team as critical to this process (unless you work for an organization where the management team really does not do much). If you do, then substitute "leaders" for "management team." I use the term "management team" to represent that group of people recognized as being responsible for the management of the organization. The management team usually is (ultimately) responsible for the management of strategic objectives. Exhibit 2.10 provides examples of objectives relating to the management team.

EXHIBIT 2.10 **STRATEGIC OBJECTIVE METRICS RELATING TO THE MANAGEMENT TEAM**

Objective	Metric
Maintain a stable management team	Turnover
Raise the quality of the management team	Analyst ratings

Processes

Processes are the predefined sets of instructions by which things get done. Exhibit 2.11 provides examples of objectives relating to processes.

EXHIBIT 2.11   **STRATEGIC OBJECTIVE METRICS RELATING TO PROCESSES**

Objective	Metric
Reduce operational errors	Count of errors
Reduce process times	Average process time

Systems

Systems are the complementary resources that exist to facilitate and support operations. Exhibit 2.12 provides examples of objectives relating to systems.

EXHIBIT 2.12   **STRATEGIC OBJECTIVE METRICS RELATING TO SYSTEMS**

Objective	Metric
Reduce complexity of information technology systems	Number of strategic suppliers
Operate systems that are more "user friendly"	"User-friendliness" survey

NOTE ON THE INTERDEPENDENCE OF OBJECTIVES

Regardless of how you categorize the strategic objectives of your organization, it is unlikely that you will be able to define mutually exclusive objectives. Rather, it is highly likely that striving to achieve one objective will have some impact on your attempts to achieve another objective. For example, outcomes of financial objectives—or, you might say, financial outcomes—are very often a secondary outcome of achievement of (or failure to achieve) some other objective. In some cases, it is a bit chicken and egg and therefore hard to tell—and it probably does not matter. Consider, for example, a decision to grow market share (a market objective). If we achieve it while keeping all other things equal, we can imagine an increase in revenue and probably profit (likely impacting one or more financial objectives). Or imagine a strategy to hire and retain the best people (an operational objective); that probably means higher salaries (and again will likely impact one or more financial objectives). The point is that strategic objectives are rarely independent, and you must be aware of the relationships. You can achieve this awareness by analyzing the strategy map, discussed later, during our discussion on cause-and-effect analysis in Chapter 6.

CHAPTER 3

At-Risk Concept

Readers familiar with the value–at–risk concept, or something similar, should skip this chapter and move on to Chapter 4.

The at-risk concept requires some understanding of commonly understood statistical concepts. If you do not care to get into the numbers part of the enterprise risk management methodology, then just think of the at-risk concept as being closely related to our earlier definition of risk: a distribution of outcomes of varying probability.

The at-risk concept boils down to identifying a point or points within the universe of possible outcomes. J.P. Morgan made the at-risk concept popular through the promotion of their value at risk methodology in 1994.[1] Soon after that methodology was publicized, a host of other parties, delighted with the approach, jumped on the at-risk concept and threw some more sophisticated statistical techniques and considerably more computer processing power in the mix to come up with a simulation approach for determining the at-risk measure. Now it is very common to find organizations using Monte Carlo or historical simulation to determine a set of possible outcomes (typically tens of thousands, sometimes millions) to understand their risk profile. The classic application, as intended when the methodology was published, is the measurement of market risk in bank trading book portfolios. In this situation, the at-risk concept answers the question: How much money could I lose over a certain time period, measured at a certain level of confidence? The question we will pose is: What is the distribution of possible outcomes we face? and the answer is not a single point from the distribution, it is the entire distribution. We will be applying the at-risk concept without strict adherence to the statistical process, in essence removing the typical standards that quantitative analysts strive to uphold. In some cases we will be so bold as to imagine (as opposed to anything more scientific) the distribution of possible outcomes.

We will now cover the basics of distributions, starting from the very simple and getting only slightly more complex. Although the discussion is restricted to simple examples, I do not wish to belittle the concept or give you the impression that what we are discussing is trivial. An understanding of probability distributions is absolutely fundamental to the successful operation of the SOAR methodology. If, for some bizarre reason, you decide not to apply the SOAR methodology, I urge you to embrace the probability distribution as the most valuable tool for risk measurement and your key to successful achievement of your strategic objectives.

A Very Simple Distribution

When you roll a (fair) six-sided die, you will get one of six outcomes: The number that ends up on top will be either 1, 2, 3, 4, 5, or . . . you guessed it . . . 6. If you roll the die enough (say a gazillion) times, you would expect to get the same number of each outcome. Expressed another way, the outcomes have equal probability. The distribution of outcomes when the die is rolled many times could be plotted as shown in Exhibit 3.1.

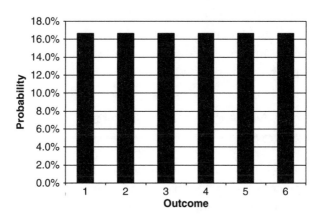

EXHIBIT 3.1   **DISTRIBUTION OF OUTCOMES OF EQUAL PROBABILITY**

Also consider the case where the die is rolled too few times. Imagine you rolled the die just twice and happened to get a 1 and a 2. Imagine you then conclude that the possible outcomes of a future role are represented by the graph in Exhibit 3.2.

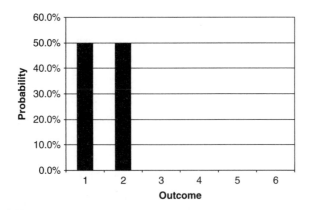

EXHIBIT 3.2   DISTRIBUTION DRAWN ON TOO FEW SAMPLES

Using the die as an example, it seems obvious that a sample of two observations is too few. You might think it seems ridiculous that someone might do something like this, but I have seen it happen, although not with a die. We will talk later about how to draw distributions of possible (future) outcomes—in fact, in Chapter 9, during our discussion of the react step of the SOAR process, we will build the distribution of possible outcomes via historical simulation. Drawing distributions of observed outcomes is a simple task, so we do not need to cover that. Rather we will spend time considering how to draw distributions of possible future outcomes.

A Slightly More Interesting Distribution

Imagine it is midsummer in California and someone asks you what you think the temperature will be tomorrow. In the absence of any news of some impending significant meteorological event, you would probably predict that it is going to be pretty similar to today, right? If you tried to get a bit more sophisticated in your prediction, you might say something like "Well, it's 100 degrees today, I reckon it's pretty likely to be around 100 tomorrow, though there's a bit of a chance that it could dip to 80." If you plotted that (imaginary) distribution, it might look something like Exhibit 3.3.

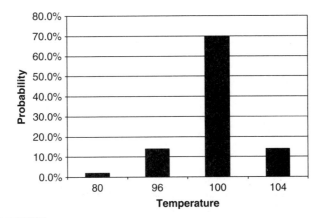

EXHIBIT 3.3   **DISTRIBUTION OF OUTCOMES OF UNEQUAL PROBABILITY**

In the distribution in Exhibit 3.3, four possible outcomes have been included. The probabilities associated with temperatures of 96, 100, and 104 represent the statement "I reckon it's pretty likely to be around 100 tomorrow." The probability assigned to the temperature of 80 aligns with the words "a bit of a chance." (Everyone knows that a "chance" equals 10% and a "bit" equals 20%, so "a bit of a chance" equals 2%, right?)

Imagine now that we increased the number of possible outcomes to, say, 4 million. Do not worry about how we do it, just imagine we do it and that the distribution of possible outcomes now looks something like Exhibit 3.4.

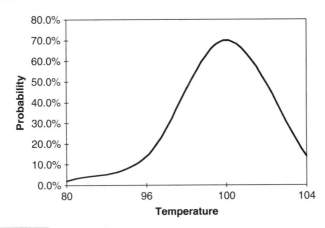

EXHIBIT 3.4   **SIMULATED DISTRIBUTION OF OUTCOMES**

Although we have increased the number of observations (or possible outcomes) from 4 to 4 million, we have kept the general shape of the distribution the same. What we have done is introduce some granularity that we simply did not specify in the original statement of our prediction. Originally we predicted that the temperature could dip to 80; an inference is that we believed there was some chance that the temperature could dip to 81. The plot in Exhibit 3.4 has simply filled in the possible outcomes of temperature tomorrow that we did not state and assigned a corresponding probability. Without knowing a great deal about statistics, you should be able to make some general remarks based on Exhibit 3.4, including:

- It is more likely to be warmer than 96 than cooler.
- There is a really small chance it will be 80 to 81.
- There is a pretty small chance it will be above 103.
- The most likely temperature is 100.

Now let us apply some imagination and consider the distribution of possible outcomes we might face when our objective is to get our stock price up to $35 per share. Imagine that the distribution of possible outcomes of the future price looks something like that shown in Exhibit 3.5.

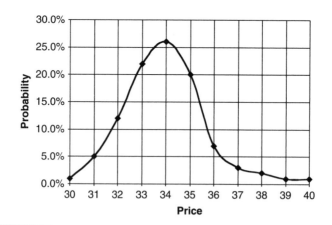

EXHIBIT 3.5   DISTRIBUTION OF OUTCOMES OF FUTURE SHARE PRICE

Some observations that can be made from this plot:

- $35 is *not* the most likely outcome ($34 is; it has a probability of 26%. There is a 20% probability that the future price will be $35.)

- The probability of an outcome in excess of $35 is 14% (i.e., the sum of 7%, 3%, 2%, 1%, and 1% for the higher outcomes). In making that statement, I am referring only to the discrete price values marked $36, $37, and so on and assuming that partial-dollar values are not possible.)

- The probability of an outcome of $35 or less is 86%.

- The average of the possible outcomes (or, in other words, the expected outcome or mean) is just less than $34. (You cannot determine that from the graph directly; you have to do the math with the numbers.)

Assuming we have no intention to manipulate the market or apply any other dirty tricks to achieve our aim, one of the roles of the enterprise risk management office is to consider whether the shape of the distribution can be manipulated through execution (and [risk] management) of appropriate strategies. We might, for example, attempt to create a distribution that looks more like the one shown in Exhibit 3.6.

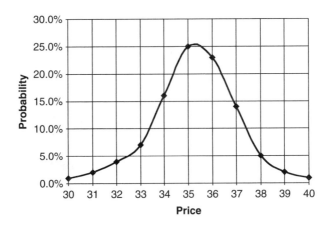

EXHIBIT 3.6   ALTERNATE DISTRIBUTION OF OUTCOMES OF FUTURE SHARE PRICE

Now let us draw observations similar to those we drew for Exhibit 3.5:

- $35 *is* the most likely outcome.
- The probability of an outcome in excess of $35 is 45% (i.e., the sum of 23%, 14%, 5%, 2%, and 1% for the higher outcomes).
- The probability of an outcome of $35 or less is 55%.
- The average of the possible outcomes (or, in other words, the expected outcome or mean) is a little over $35 (again, do the math).

Clearly, if we are able to create a set of circumstances that means we face this second set of possible outcomes, we have added value, even if we do not then continue to help manage the risks the organization faces as it strives to achieve its target share price. However, we *would* continue to help the organization achieve that aim. In theory, at least, we have made our lives easier by improving the risk profile from the outset.

We can think of the plot shown in Exhibit 3.5 as representing the inherent risk and that shown in Exhibit 3.6 as representing the residual risk. We can see the impact of the risk mitigation we have applied by plotting the two distributions, as shown in Exhibit 3.7. This is one way to view the impact of risk mitigation, or controls.

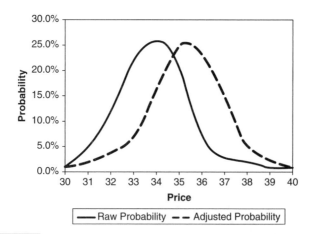

EXHIBIT 3.7   COMPARISON OF THE DISTRIBUTIONS OF OUTCOMES OF FUTURE SHARE PRICE

An important point for you to take from this chapter is that risk can be represented by the distribution of possible outcomes that may eventuate

(due to the presence of that risk or those risks). In other words, that a range
of outcomes is possible evidences the presence of risk. When you think of
risk represented as a distribution of possible outcomes, you should think of
these elements:

- The fact that a distribution of possible outcomes exists is evidence of
  risk. (The corollary to this statement is that the presence of risk
  means the existence of various outcomes.)

- The distribution shows the outcome (or impact or severity) on one
  axis (usually the horizontal) and the probability (or likelihood) on the
  other (usually the vertical axis).

- You cannot directly measure risk(s) from the distribution; you can
  only measure the degree of variation in outcomes caused by the presence of risk(s). You can use the measure of variation in outcomes as a
  proxy for a measure of risk.

Exhibit 3.8 presents some distributions of possible outcomes.

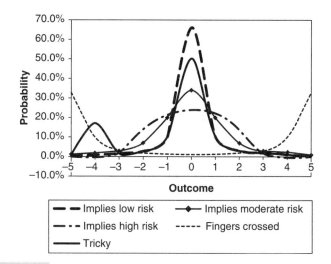

**EXHIBIT 3.8   SOME EXAMPLES OF DISTRIBUTIONS OF POSSIBLE
OUTCOMES**

Assume that the "outcome" on the horizontal axis represents (possible)
deviation from the desired or target value (representing achievement of a

strategic objective). The probability of the outcome is shown on the vertical axis. The tallest, thinnest distribution (shown with a dashed line) is the one that implies the lowest risk, as the vast majority of possible outcomes are not far away from the target. The low, wide distribution (shown with a dotted and dashed line) implies relatively high risk, as there is no significant tendency toward the target. The inverse distribution, which dips in the middle and rises at both ends, offers little hope of achieving the objective as it shows decreasing likelihood (probability) of values as you approach the target. If you face this sort of distribution after doing your best to create favorable circumstances (i.e., this distribution represents the residual risk), it might be time to update your curriculum vitae. The double-humped distribution (shown with the solid line) poses significant challenge. It shows that, for some reason, there is a significant chance (or probability) of an adverse outcome. That is bad news. Even worse, it is not matched by a significant chance of a positive outcome. Further investigation is needed to determine the causes behind these possible adverse outcomes. As the enterprise risk management officer, your goal is to create a set of circumstances that produces the tallest, thinnest distribution (around your target) of possible outcomes for the organization.

LOCATION OF THE DISTRIBUTION

In the last section, I used the phrase "around your target," which requires a little more attention. You are now familiar with the concepts of height and width. The third vital parameter of the distribution of possible outcomes is location. Under the SOAR (Set Observe Analyze React) process, we define (within the set step) a single metric to represent the strategic objective. At the outset, we determine the value of that metric that equates to achieving our objective. You may have already guessed, or perhaps just assumed, that the position of the distribution you strive to create (Note: You do not actually create the distribution; you create the set of circumstances that supports the distribution) should consider the target value of the metric. This point has been implicit in the example relating to share price, so I will use that one again. In that example, we strived to achieve a share price of $35 and we managed to create a set of circumstances that resulted in the distribution of possible outcomes shown in Exhibit 3.9.

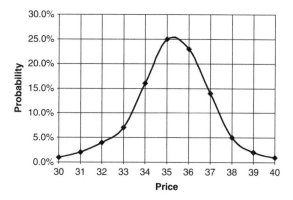

EXHIBIT 3.9   **DISTRIBUTION OF OUTCOMES OF FUTURE SHARE PRICE**

These observations were made regarding the distribution:

- $35 (our target) is the most likely outcome (the mode).

- The probability of an outcome in excess of (our target) $35 is 45% (i.e., the sum of 23%, 14%, 5%, 2%, and 1% for the higher outcomes).

- The probability of an outcome of $35 (our target) or less is 55%.

- The average of the possible outcomes (or, in other words, the expected outcome or mean) is a little over (our target) $35.

Now imagine that we can create a set of circumstances that results in a distribution of the same shape (which we have described by height and width) but a different location, such as the one that appears in Exhibit 3.10.

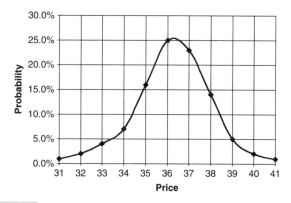

EXHIBIT 3.10   **ALTERNATE DISTRIBUTION OF OUTCOMES OF FUTURE SHARE PRICE**

From the exhibit (and the data on which it is drawn), we can make these observations:

- $36 (i.e., $1 more than our target) is the most likely outcome (the mode).
- The probability of an outcome in excess of $35 (our target) is 70% (i.e., the sum of 25%, 23%, 14%, 5%, 2%, and 1% for the higher outcomes).
- The probability of an outcome of $35 or less is 30%.
- The average of the possible outcomes (or, in other words, the expected outcome or mean) is a little over $36.

For convenience, Exhibit 3.11 shows the two distributions together.

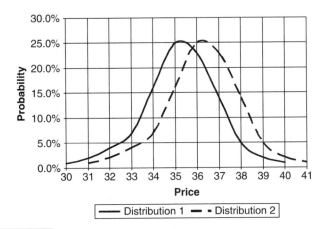

EXHIBIT 3.11   **COMPARISON OF THE DISTRIBUTIONS OF OUTCOMES OF FUTURE SHARE PRICE**

The point to keep in mind is that both the shape and the location of the distribution are important. The two distributions have the same shape, but because they boast different locations, they represent different risk.

BASIC STATISTICAL MEASURES

Every enterprise risk management officer should understand the meaning of these basic statistical measures:

Minimum   The smallest value within a set of numbers

Maximum   The largest value within a set of numbers

Mean   Calculated as the sum of a set of numbers divided by the count of numbers in the set

Mode   The number that appears most frequently in a set of numbers. In a probability distribution, the mode is the outcome that has the highest probability

Standard Deviation   A measure of how widely the numbers in a set of numbers vary from the mean. In a probability distribution, standard deviation describes how wide the distribution is

Skew   Tells us whether numbers greater than the mean are more or less likely than numbers less than the mean. In other words, skew relates to the symmetry of the distribution

In addition to the basic measures, you should completely understand the only-slightly-more-complex at-risk measure.

AT-RISK MEASURE

The at-risk measure is simply some point in the distribution. It has a value and a probability. An at-risk measure is often selected as a sort of worst-case result. You might say something like "I am 99% sure that the result will not be worse than X." In that statement, "X" is the value of the at-risk measure. Saying "There is a 1% probability that the result will be worse than X" refers to the same point on the distribution. The term "at risk" is used as the name for this measure to remind us of its origin. (Well, not really the origin of the measure, but the source of its fame.)

Take a quick look at a series of numbers, the statistical measures associated with those numbers, and the probability distribution that can be drawn from them.

Series

```
-10,-10,-10,-7,-7,-5,-5,-5,-3,-3,-3,-3,0,0,0,0,
  0,0,3,3,3,3,5,5,5,7,7,10
Minimum = -10
Maximum = 10
Mean = sum(series)/count(series) = -20/28 = -0.7(ish)
Mode = 0
Standard deviation = 5.5(ish)
```

Skew = −0.1

At−risk measure = There is a 3 in 28 chance that the out−
come will be worse than −7.

What does the probability distribution look like? Most of it looks like a "normal" distribution, but there is a bit of a lump in the left-hand tail, as shown in Exhibit 3.12.

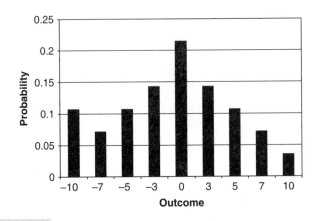

EXHIBIT 3.12   MOSTLY NORMAL DISTRIBUTION

What do the statistical measures really mean? Consider each one in the context of the distribution from which they come.

The most misunderstood value is the mean. Take a moment to think about what a probability distribution is: the distribution of values of some-thing. Within the context of enterprise risk management, the distribution might show the distribution of observed (i.e., historical) values, or it might show the distribution of predicted (future) values. Mean is easily understood when we are thinking of observed values, but it is very often misinterpreted when we are talking about predicted values. Consider the example series, which boasts a mean of −0.7. Imagine that the number series is the output of a model that forecasts the number of people who will join the organiza-tion next month. A negative value does not mean the people who join are bad; rather it means that people leave rather than join. According to the model that produced the number series, there is a 3 out of 28 chance that 10 people will leave next month.

The mean is often referred to as the "expected" value, and this is the term I feel is most often misunderstood. There are two common misinterpretations of this term/number. Often people think the expected value is the one that is most likely to occur. It is not. The number that is most likely to occur is called the mode, and it is simply the one with the highest probability. In the distribution given, the mode is 0. The other very common misinterpretation of this number is that it is possible. Very often it is not. In our example, as I mentioned, the mean is −0.7. But it is impossible that 0.7 people leave. There has never been a month in the past (28 months) where 0.7 people have left, and there never will be in the future. The −0.7 simply means that the average number of people who have left over the past 28 months is −0.7. Or it means that the average of the forecast values for next month is −0.7, depending on whether the number series represents observed or forecast values. So how should you use the mean? You should present the mean with a suitable note assigned to it. If in the example here the number series represents the forecast number of people who will join next month, you might list number −0.7 in a report and note that "−0.7 is the average of the 28 predictions of the number of people to join next month."

If someone said to you, "You have to pick one number out of those 28. If you pick the number of people who join next month I will give you 100 bucks," what number would you pick? Before answering, we should modify the number series by replacing one of those −10s with a −100 (representing December last year, when 100 people left due to poor bonuses). So now the distribution is:

```
−100,−10,−10,−7,−7,−5,−5,−5,−3,−3,−3,
  −3,0,0,0,0,0,0,3,3,3,3,5,5,5,7,7,10
```

The summary statistics are:

Minimum = −100

Maximum = 10

Mean = −3.2

Mode = 0

Standard deviation = 19.5

Skew = −4.7

The distribution is shown in Exhibit 3.13.

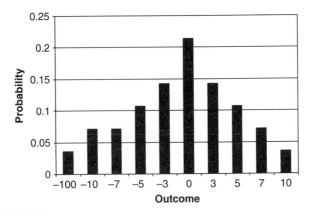

EXHIBIT 3.13   **ANOTHER MOSTLY NORMAL DISTRIBUTION**

What number would you choose? If you chose anything other than 0, you need to review this section. If you have reviewed this section and still believe something other than 0 is the right answer, consider this example: Imagine you are playing roulette and have only two choices: You can choose from either red or black, or you can choose any one of the 37 numbers. Choosing one of the 37 numbers gives you a 1 in 37 chance of winning, right? Choosing red or black gives you 18 chances out of 37. (For those who are not familiar with the roulette wheel, 0 is green and 1 to 36 are either red or black.) Now go back to our previous number series; if you choose 0, you have a 6 out of 28 chance of being correct. No other choice gives you such a high chance of wining.

What else can we observe from the distribution and/or interpret from the summary statistics of the original number series?

The graph shown in Exhibit 3.12 and the skew tell us that the distribution is skewed (or biased) toward the negative values. This means we face an uphill battle; the chance of a negative outcome is higher than the chance of a positive one. Before I go on, I need to clarify that last statement. In some cases, a higher value does not necessarily represent a positive outcome. In the example we are currently using, we have not talked about the target value for the metric and we have not identified good and bad outcomes. In saying the chance of a negative outcome is higher than the chance of a positive one, I am assuming that the target value is 0, negative values represent negative outcomes, and positive values represent positive outcomes.

Exhibit 3.12 and the associated standard deviation tell us that the distribution is spread quite widely (i.e., values quite far from the mean are reasonably likely). I need to clarify this sentence too. I have deliberately used a couple of subjective terms, namely "quite" and "reasonably." This is because standard deviation is a measure that makes most sense when two or more distributions are compared. As you can see from Exhibits 3.12 and 3.13 and the two associated number series, the distributions are very similar, apart from one observation (or forecast). In the second series, we replaced one of the −10s with a −100. This change impacted the minimum, the mean, the standard deviation, and the skew. By comparing the summary statistics of the two number series, we can get a better appreciation of how each summary statistic helps describe the distribution.

When examining numbers and summary or descriptive statistics like these, keep them in context. Doing so will help you interpret the numbers correctly. Continuing with the previous examples, if you were told that the expected number of people to join next month is −0.7, you would ask "Does that mean that the average of the predictions is −0.7 and so we predict that 1 person will leave next month?" You need to judge whether the summary statistics have meaning. Recently I heard a statement that I thought was a great example of how summary statistics can be less than helpful, even misleading: On average, every person on earth has one testicle. The statement is statistically correct and practically useless.

■ NOTE

1. For more information, including a copy of the technical document detailing direct application of the value-at-risk concept to the measurement of risk associated with the trading book of a bank, you can visit the RiskMetrics Group's Web site, www.riskmetrics.com/index.jsp.

CHAPTER 4

SOAR (the Methodology): Strategic Objectives at Risk

The strategic objectives at risk (SOAR) methodology comprises some of the concepts of the now-famous value-at-risk methodology of J. P. Morgan, mentioned in Chapter 3. It is from the J. P. Morgan methodology that I borrow the at-risk phrase. The SOAR methodology simply applies an at-risk measurement approach, as described earlier, to measures of outcomes of strategic objectives. As you now know, that means the methodology involves consideration of possible outcomes and associated probabilities. And as you can see, it is really very simple; for each of your strategic objectives, define the possible outcomes and calculate a probability for each of those outcomes. Unfortunately, like most things in life, the devil is in the details. The SOAR methodology follows the SOAR process, as detailed throughout most of the rest of this book.

SOAR METHODOLOGY COMPONENTS

In this chapter, I describe the components of the SOAR methodology. Fundamental to it is the SOAR process—the major focus of this book. The other elements, described next, although critical for successful application of the method, are not unique to the SOAR methodology, and so they are not covered in great detail. Because these other elements are already in common usage, you can find much more information on these subjects than I could hope to provide.

Strategic Objectives

Statements of strategic objectives are the starting point of the SOAR methodology. Application of the SOAR process will highlight poorly defined or poorly stated objectives in the very early stages of the process. Similarly, in its early stages, the process may identify a need to review objectives, where the uncertainty associated with achieving an objective is deemed unacceptable.

As mentioned, I am a fan of the SMART expression of objectives. In particular, the "measurable" element gives us our starting point for the determination of metrics. I offer here some examples of statements of strategic objectives found in publicly available documents and describe how the SOAR process would assess these statements. I do this to draw your attention to the importance of well-defined statements of objectives, not to offer guidance on setting or stating strategic objectives.

Statement 1

> Our goal is to be the world's premier alternative investment platform and we have a unique business model designed to accomplish that objective.

> —CITIGROUP ANNUAL REPORT, 2005

By the way, remember I spoke earlier of having a little fun by asking "Why (are you trying to achieve that)?" I urge you to consider why the objectives presented here might have been set and whether some other objective might have been more suitable. Let us play with this first one together. The objective is "to be the world's premier alternative investment platform." Why would a company want to achieve that? I doubt it is so that management can place the trophy on a shelf. Could it be for marketing reasons? Yes, I think it could. But if so, is the company's objective really to attract new business, and is being number one a way to do that? Maybe it is something else. Maybe it is because being "premier" means the company has delivered the best average annual performance over the preceding five years. If so, is its objective to deliver the best average annual performance over five years? I am not just playing around; by asking "Why," we actually get a better understanding of the objective and that is very important.

Let us move on. A positive within this statement is that the "measurable" part is easily identifiable; the company aims to be number one in its field. However, we cannot immediately define a metric for this strategic objective, as the measure of "premier" is neither explicit nor obvious. Does it relate to new customers acquired over a certain period, to the number of customers at the end of a certain period, to the value of business conducted with customers, to customer satisfaction, to investment returns, or to something else? What will make this organization "premier"?

Missing from the statement of this strategic objective is the time frame. Without a time frame, it would be impossible to conceive the distribution of possible outcomes required under the SOAR process.

Just as an aside, I do not think statements of strategic objectives should go beyond (or fall short of) stating the objective. Accordingly, I would drop the second half of that statement, as it relates to the resources that are going to be employed to achieve the objective.

A more appealing statement of this strategic objective would be:

> Our goal is to have funds under management that exceed any of our competitors in alternative investment platforms by at least 5% by the end of 2008.

Statement 2

> . . . strive for improvements in health care and fairer access in a world where life expectancy ranges from 85 years in Japan to just 36 years in Sierra Leone.

—World Health Organization, "Working for Health – An Introduction to the World Health Organization," 2006

I know I said we would only do it for the first one, but I cannot resist, so let us ask "Why?" again. This organization's objective is to "strive for improvements." Why would it want to do that? Well, my guess is that it actually wants to *make* improvements. In my view this statement of a strategic objective falls well short of the mark. If you take this one literally, the organization can achieve the objective simply by *trying* to deliver something. How slack is that? Imagine if it gives absolutely no thought to how it will "strive for improvements" and decides to raise the salaries of health care workers on the basis that "you get what you pay for." The organization imagines that salary increases will result in improvements in the overall system. Maybe it will, maybe it will not. Has the organization strived? Well, its leaders might argue they have. So has the organization achieved the stated objective? Again, it might argue that it has. A more suitable statement might be something like:

> Reduce patient average waiting times by 10% per annum over the next 5 years and deliver, within 25 years, equivalent per-capita medical services to developing countries as currently available in developed nations.

Statement 3

> Our aim is to improve the quality of life for our residents and businesses.

Quality of life (QOL)—we all know how measurable that is, right? Just use the QOL meter. However, the fact that something is difficult to measure does not and should not prevent it, i.e., the "something," from being the outcome we want to achieve. I will refer to this next quote a few times in this book:

> *Measure all that can be measured and render measurable all that defies measurement.*

> —GALILEO GALILEI, 1564–1642

Seeking to measurably improve the quality of life for residents is reasonable, but do businesses really enjoy a quality of life? They do not; they are just legal constructs that do not have lives. A better statement of the two distinct objectives of this organization might be:

> To increase rail services by 10% and park areas by 15% over two years.
> To increase the number of businesses in the district by 10% over 5 years.

Statement 4

> Provide the mineral industry with world-leading capabilities leading to breakthroughs in exploration in Australia's extensive areas of regolith cover.

> —COOPERATIVE RESEARCH CENTRE FOR LANDSCAPE ENVIRONMENTS AND MINERAL EXPLORATION (HTTP:// CRCLEME.ORG.AU/ABOUT/OBJECTIVES.HTML)

This statement seems pretty reasonable to me, though not perfect. There is no time constraint, and it should not include a reference to an outcome that seems to be beyond the control of the organization. Really, the company's objective is to provide world-leading capabilities, and it *hopes* that these capabilities will be used by participants in the mineral industry (customers) to make breakthroughs.

Statement 5

> To maximize retention, achievement, and success.

> —TAMESIDE COLLEGE (WWW.TAMESIDE.AC.UK/
> CORPORATION/STRATEGIC.ASP)

This one really is a cracker. I particularly dislike the use of "maximize"; what does that mean? It annoys me when organizations make statements like "maximize returns"; they are just so . . . empty! What is it that this organization wants to retain? It is an educational institution, so we can imagine that it wants to retain students or teachers (or both), but this really needs to be explicit. Maybe it wants to retain rainwater for drinking. I do not really see much point in attempting to restate this one; the organization would be better off going back to the drawing board and figuring out what it is it wants to achieve. Really, "maximize achievement"—what does that mean?

Statement 6

> Secure the United States from direct attack.

> —GLOBALSECURITY.ORG (WWW.GLOBALSECURITY.ORG/
> MILITARY/LIBRARY/POLICY/DOD/
> NDS–USA_MAR2005_II.HTM)

Wow, good luck! I will let you consider this one free of sarcastic comment from me.

Statement 7

> Our aim is to be Australia's number one retailer in all our brands by delighting our customers, growing our shareholder value, and being the best team.

> —COLES MYER LTD (WWW.COLESMYER.COM/INVESTORS/)

As is remarkably typical of statements of strategic objectives, this one has some of the SMART elements and lacks others, meaning that it is not well defined for our purpose (and, I would argue, for those who have to determine the strategic plan). On the positive side, the statement provides some indicators, in the "by" statement, for setting metrics: "delighting our customers," "growing our shareholder value," and "being the best team." But it is not possible to go straight to metrics; a restatement of the objective (after a little thought) is required. How "delighted" does the organization wish its customers to be? Extremely? Somewhat? Is "extremely happy" as good as delighted? And in what ways does it want its customers to be delighted? By the low prices, the wide aisles, the ease of parking, or the complimentary glass of champagne on entry? By pointing out that the "by" statement implies metrics, I am not suggesting that inclusion of such a statement is a good thing. In fact, I am opposed to it. The statement of a strategic objective should be just that: the statement of an objective. It should be a statement of what the organization wishes to achieve, absent any indication of how it plans to achieve it. What if this organization achieves its ambition to be Australia's number-one retailer through some other means; will it be satisfied? This one could be restated as:

Our aim is to be Australia's number one retailer by the end of 2008.

When the SOAR process is applied, one of the questions that would be asked early on is "What metrics do we apply for the measurement of 'number one'?" (Questions like this are raised in the set step of the SOAR process.) In answering that question, discussions about "delighting our customers," "growing our shareholder value," and "the best team" will arise.

When I began searching for some public statements of strategic objectives, I had hoped to present some that required refinement and some that had immediate application to the SOAR process. Regrettably, I was unable to find any that fit the second category. This came as somewhat of a surprise to me. For sure, I held an expectation that the vast majority of statements would fail to meet the SMART criteria, but I had expected to find at least a few that would meet them. I imagine that the public statement of a strategic objective differs somewhat from that by which strategic plans are conjured and that my failure to uncover a suitably articulated statement of strategic objective is a result of my decision to seek statements available in the public domain. For example, if a bank's objective is to increase profit by increasing the number of highly profitable customers and reducing the number of not-so-profitable customers, it is unlikely to announce that it aims "to increase profit by actively reducing the number of low-profit accounts." I suspect the objectives expressed publicly are only those that position the organization positively.

Given that I have been unable to find a well-stated strategic objective in the public domain, after many hours of searching, I have made some up. Here they are, for your consideration:

> To increase total revenue by at least 10% per annum over the next five years.
>
> To provide shareholders an average total return on investment of at least 12% per annum over 10 years.
>
> To reduce greenhouse emissions by at least 5% per annum over the next 10 years.
>
> To attract at least 100 new members this year.
>
> To lower total operating expenses by at least 5% over two years.
>
> By 2008, to be recognized as providing the best customer service.

I would like to mention my use of terms such as "at least." Implicitly, expressions like this recognize two things:

1. There is some threshold level that signifies achievement.
2. Attaining a certain value precisely is neither likely nor all that important.

For example, when a company aims to achieve sales of $500 million, it is unlikely to consider itself to have failed if it achieves sales of $505 million. Note that an expression like "at least" preserves clarity of the objective, as opposed to other expressions, such as "maximize" or "minimize," which almost defy definition and should not be used in statements of strategic objectives. In most of the examples provided, the use of "at least" could be interpreted to incorporate the notion that more is better. Indeed, in the examples, more probably *is* better, but it will not always be the case. Where an objective needs to be bound, it should be bound in the statement of the objective, such as in this example:

> We aim to maintain inflation in the range of 1% to 4% per annum over the next five years.

Execution Resources
(The Enterprise Risk Management Office)

The strategic plan(s) designed to enable the organization to achieve its strategic objective(s) should, just like a project plan, identify the human and other resources required for plan execution. In addition to those resources, a distinct set of resources is required for the execution of the SOAR process. The elements of resourcing that I would particularly like to discuss here relate to that second set of resources, those applied to the execution of the SOAR process. These resources are known collectively as the enterprise risk management office.

The enterprise risk management office will prove most successful when it is operationally independent of all other business units and has the sole purpose of executing the SOAR process. The human resources of the enterprise risk management office are vital to the success of your enterprise risk management program. In light of this, the SOAR methodology includes an education program and certification process for enterprise risk management officers, designed to ensure that these officers have a common understanding of and consistently apply the SOAR methodology. I will not go into the detail of the education program here; however, I have included some example questions from the certification exam in the appendix. Consistent application of the SOAR methodology is important to its success; the enterprise risk management office must succeed any individual enterprise risk management officer, and the objective of the education program and associated qualification is to commoditize (as much as possible) enterprise risk management officers. A second reason for advocating ownership of the SOAR methodology in a separate unit is because it is uncommon for a single group of people to be given responsibility for all strategic objectives. You could say, of course, that the board or senior management ultimately is responsible for all objectives, and you are probably right, but very often these people are too far removed to significantly influence the outcomes of the strategic plans. In this case, the enterprise risk management office really represents the execution arm of the board or senior management group. If the board or senior management does take an active role in the management of the strategic plans, then by all means let ownership of the SOAR methodology rest with it.

SOAR Process

The SOAR process is the major element of the SOAR methodology and, as such, is the main focus of this book. Chapter 5 addresses the SOAR process.

SOAR (the Process)

As presented in Chapter 4, the SOAR methodology comprises:

- The stated strategic objectives
- The enterprise risk management office
- The SOAR process

We have covered the first two components as far as I intend to. Now we are going to examine the SOAR process. The SOAR process involves:

- *Setting* metrics for each of the defined strategic objectives
- *Observing* metric values
- *Analyzing* movements in metric values
- *Reacting* to what the analyses reveal

The SOAR process may be represented as shown in Exhibit 5.1.

In the chapters that follow, we will analyze the four steps of the SOAR process. From this chapter, you only need to retain this information:

- The SOAR process comprises four steps:
  1. Set
  2. Observe
  3. Analyze
  4. React
- The SOAR process is iterative, commencing once the strategic objective has been stated and concluding at the end of the objective period.

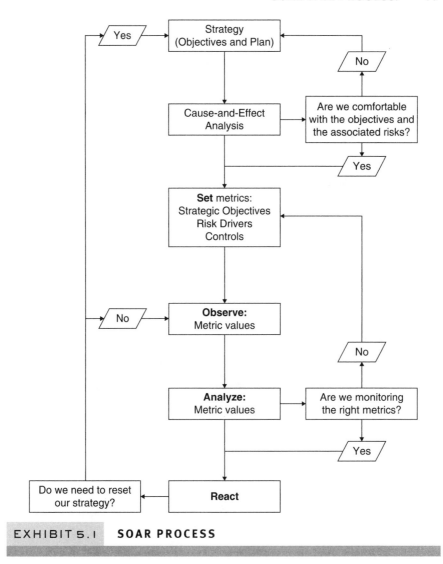

EXHIBIT 5.1   SOAR PROCESS

CHAPTER 6

Set Metrics for Defined Strategic Objectives

As I have mentioned, I have no intention of getting into the art of setting strategic objectives. Rather I will detail how to define (or set) metrics for each of your strategic objectives, assuming that you have defined the objectives already. Do not misunderstand my use of the word "set"; it does not relate to setting objectives, rather it relates to setting metrics that relate to the defined objective.

The objective of step 1 of the SOAR process, set, is to define metrics relating to each of the strategic objectives. Once the metrics are defined, step 1 demands that you determine target values for metrics. Note from the earlier discussion of SMART statements of strategic objectives that the process for defining metrics may lead you to modify or even abandon your objectives or simply to restate them. Step 1 of the SOAR process can provide valuable input for determining (or modifying) the strategic plan.

After you, the enterprise risk manager, have read the statement of the strategic objective, you must determine one or more metrics by which to manage the objective. The frequent measurement of the value of the metric(s) is critical to successful operation of both the SOAR process and the strategic plan. The natural consequence of successful execution of the strategic plan is achievement of the strategic objective. Chapter 7, which discusses step 2 of the SOAR process, observe, covers the frequent measurement of the value of the metric. For now let us consider the importance of measurement, because the fact that measurement is important means we have to *set* metrics.

WHY MEASURE?

Let me quote Galileo again:

> *Measure all that can be measured and render measurable all that defies measurement.*

—GALILEO GALILEI, 1564–1642

Measurement is absolutely fundamental to managing anything, and that, of course, includes strategic objectives. Think of a couple of things you manage every day and then consider whether you measure something in order to manage those things. One example might be your relationship with your partner. When you get home, he or she seems to be a bit grumpy and so you decide to tread carefully or maybe go straight back out for a beer. What have you done? You have measured the level of grumpiness exhibited by your partner, albeit implicitly. Or how about getting to that 8 a.m. meeting on time? Your aim is to arrive at 7:55, but you sleep through the alarm and wake 10 minutes later than planned. So you do everything a little more quickly to make up the 10 minutes lost; you measure the time and, just as you might do if you foresee failure to achieve a strategic objective, you react. The only difference between the examples I have given and the right approach to managing strategic objectives is the level of formality or discipline; the management of strategic objectives requires the application of a more formal or disciplined approach.

An old adage states that you cannot manage what you cannot measure. Measurement is the only way to be sure of your progress to date. It allows you to apply informed judgment in determining the most appropriate future actions. Measurement allows you to track where you have been and plan where you are going. When you meet an objective by some means other than by the execution of a plan to meet that objective, you should consider yourself incredibly lucky. Planning is the best way to ensure that objectives are met, and measurement is the best way to monitor how successful you are being in executing your plan.

Translating strategic objectives into target metric values is also a great way to make the objective and your progress more obvious. Although I am the first to admit that numbers can be ambiguous, I believe they are usually less ambiguous than words. I will use a few examples of statements of strategic objectives from Chapter 4 and translate them into SOAR (metric) equivalents:

> Statement 1: Our goal is to be the world's premier alternative investment platform and we have a unique business model designed to accomplish that objective.
>
> SOAR (metric) equivalent: Our goal is to be ranked first in the 2008 "Alternative Investment Platform" survey.
>
> Statement 7: Our aim is to be Australia's number one retailer in all our brands by delighting our customers, growing our shareholder value, and being the best team.
>
> SOAR (metric) equivalent: Our aim is to be ranked first in the 2008 "Retailer of the Year" competition.

Do you see how much clearer the objective is when stated in SOAR equivalents, and how much more easily progress can be tracked? Right now it might be a bit of a stretch to see how much more easily progress can be tracked, but it will be clear soon. Reread the first statement and imagine you want to visually represent where you are today and where you want to be in the future. From Statement 1, you have only one helpful word: "premier." The translation of the statement into a SOAR (metric) equivalent presents a few useful words: "ranked first" and " '2008 Alternative Investment Platform survey.' " As you can see, when expressed in a SOAR (metric) fashion, the goal becomes much clearer. We can read exactly what we want to achieve, and we can read the measurement that will be applied to judge us. What would you do if you were asked to plot a graph representing the two statements of the same strategic objective? The expression in SOAR (metric) terminology would be easier to plot, right?

CLASSES OF METRICS

I advocate classifying metrics into three categories. Although applying a classification may be confusing and is often a redundant, time-consuming, and argument-provoking exercise, I believe that by considering three different classes of metrics, you are more likely to think of things that can help you measure your progress toward achievement of your objectives from different angles. You are also more likely to think of each of the contributing forces more carefully. I do not mind if you end up deciding that you do not know whether a metric should fall into category A or B or concluding that you cannot identify a risk indicator metric. That you have spent time trying is the important part. In most cases, you will have little difficulty determining the right metric for each class. In those cases where classification seems troublesome, it is probably not the classification system causing the difficulty; it is probably ambiguity in the objective. If so, clarify the objective first. I propose these three classes of metrics:

1. Strategic objective metrics
2. Risk driver metrics
3. Control metrics

Metrics for Strategic Objectives

A strategic objective must have at least one metric and may have several metrics associated with it. In order to manage strategic objectives successfully, it is important that you can monitor progress with relative ease. To this end, the SOAR methodology always reduces measurement to a single metric for each objective. So if you set yourself four strategic objectives, the SOAR methodology ultimately will guide you to the calculation of four metrics. To avoid confusion, I will refer to these as strategic objective metrics. When defining strategic objective metrics, look for the measurable part of the objective when expressed in a SMART manner; this will give you a great starting point for determining appropriate metrics. I say "starting point" for two reasons. The first reason is because, as we have seen, the metric for the strategic objective is not always apparent from the statement of strategic objective. Take this one as an example:

> Statement 3: Our aim is to improve the quality of life for our residents and businesses.

It is clear that we will need to consider and define an appropriate metric that measures quality of life. No such metric exists. However, as with most things, something similar probably does exist, and we can, at the very least, consider that existing thing before we try to create something completely new. For quality of life, the first thing that comes to mind is the measurement of standard of living. Another thing that comes to mind is the measurement of water quality.

The second reason I refer to the statement of strategic objective as the starting point for determining metrics is because I recommend you create a number of metrics, at least one from each class.

Metrics for Risk Drivers

I have no doubt that at least 50% of readers who have reached this point will start to question the sense of categorizing metrics into classes. Remember my rationale: It is to get you to think about all of the things that influence the outcome of your actions as you strive toward achievement of your strategic objectives and to do so from different points of view. It is a bit like using your eyes and ears when you cross the road. Must you use both senses to cross the road? Obviously not—blind people and deaf people manage to cross roads safely. In doing so, they rely more heavily on their remaining senses than people who have the luxury of both sight and hearing. That said, who do you think faces the more dangerous situation? Note that the increase in risk (or danger) is not due to a change in external or environmental factors; it is due to differences in approach. Similarly, you can define metrics relating to your strategic objectives without applying the classification proposed here. I would urge you not to take that shortcut, however, for a simple reason: An attempt to classify the metrics you come up with or to define at least one metric per class will give you the greatest chance of identifying *all* relevant metrics.

Metrics for risk drivers are quite often referred to as key risk indicators (KRIs) or early warning indicators (EWIs). They are predictors, or leading indicators, of risk. Measurement and monitoring of KRIs is absolutely essential to the successful management of strategic objectives. KRI measurement will almost certainly allow a proactive approach to risk management as opposed to a reactive one. With the right KRI monitoring processes in place, an organization should be able to minimize the possibility and/or impact of events that may adversely impact its ability to meet strategic objectives. In addition to managing risk through KRIs, the application of appropriate controls enhances an organization's ability to minimize the possibility and/or impact of events.

Soon we will examine methods for determining metrics of all classes. For now, let me present an example of a risk driver metric (or KRI or EWI, whatever you want to call it) for one of our example statements of strategic objective.

Statement 3: Our aim is to improve the quality of life for our residents and businesses.

When we set the risk driver metric, we are identifying something that indicates that we are straying from or, even better, *likely* to stray from our target value for our strategic objective metric. Of course, we will measure the actual value of our strategic objective metric frequently throughout the objective period; however, we use the risk driver metric as an advance warning that the next measurement of the strategic objective metric might not be favorable.

Indicators often are classified as either leading or lagging indicators. It should be obvious that we are looking to identify *leading* indicators. We want to identify risk (and control) indicator metrics that are predictive of the strategic objective metric.

Without explaining how I have determined the metric (we will examine methods for setting metrics in just a second), let me propose one for now. I propose that the risk driver metric for the strategic objective just mentioned be the number of complaints about services and that it be measured monthly.

Metrics for Controls

As we have discussed, controls are safeguards that the organization has put in place in order to minimize the probability of an event occurring or to lessen the impact of an event if it does occur. It is vital that control metrics (or control indicators) be employed such that the organization can validate its risk mitigation strategies; that is, the organization must put in place processes that try to mitigate risk, and it must examine those processes in order to ensure that they are both well conceived/designed and well executed. Think of controls you may have put in place for your day-to-day life. You may have purchased medical insurance, for example. Does this reduce the likelihood of getting ill or suffering personal injury? Absolutely not. The insurance reduces the cost of medical expenses for medical services that bring you back to good health following injury or illness. In other words, it reduces the impact or severity of an event, should it happen. Let us say that you get hit by a car and suffer a couple of broken bones. An ambulance shows up and offers to take you to the nearest hospital. You accept. Two months later the ambulance service provider sends you a bill. You call your medical insurance provider only to learn that ambulance services are not covered. Is that a fault in execution? No, the insurance is provided (or not, as the case may be) as per design. In hindsight, you should have paid the additional premium to get greater coverage. Now, had you "tested" the control at some time prior to your accident, you might have learned that your coverage was inadequate. In this example, the test could be as simple as calling your insurer and asking "Does my insurance cover ambulance services?"

Let us continue with the example strategic objective and define the control metric.

> Statement 3: Our aim is to improve the quality of life for our residents and businesses.

Again, I will not explain how I have determined the metric just yet. I propose that the control metric for this strategic objective be the number of times services have been tested by the enterprise risk management office during the month and that it be measured on a monthly basis. (In the case of both risk driver and control metrics, when I say "services," I am referring to things like waste management services, electricity, water, and postal services.)

SETTING METRICS

So how do you define the relevant metrics for each strategic objective? It should be pretty easy to define metrics in the metrics for strategic objectives class by examining the "measurable" part from the SMART statement of the strategic objective. When I say "easy," I am not suggesting that the choice of metric will always be obvious. As the enterprise risk manager, you have to *make* it easy. You can make it as difficult as you like. Consider this example. Imagine the objective is "to increase profit by 10%." There is obviously some need to clarify the definition of profit (before or after tax, including or excluding depreciation, etc.), but apart from that, you should be close to setting "profit" as your strategic objective metric. Where you can *make* it more difficult is by considering the desirability of various outcomes. That would involve determining whether 11% was more desirable than 10% and 12% more desirable than 11%, and so forth. Then you would have to determine which level of the metric (now including the desirability element) should be the target value. There is no need to go down that path in this case. Just set the metric to "growth in profit" and set the target value to 10% *or more*. An alternative is to use dollar equivalents. When deciding which to use (percent or dollars), you would choose the one that the people who are interested in the outcome understand more readily.

For risk drivers and controls, the best way to define metrics is to conduct an analysis to determine everything that influences the outcome of your objective. For some people, such an exercise could take more than a lifetime. Trust me; that is too long. If you are one of those people, you need to simplify in order to conduct the analysis in a reasonable time. (Or you go get the coffee and let someone else sort it out while you are gone.)

Let us try to think of something that seems like a complex strategic objective with myriad influences and then set about determining an adequate set of metrics for it. Imagine your organization aims to reduce the emission of greenhouse gases worldwide by 25% over the next 10 years. You are the director of enterprise risk management, charged with (among other things) applying a monitoring process that will give the organization the greatest chance of obtaining its objective. There is only one way to go: Immerse yourself in a cause-and-effect analysis. I will describe it here, then we will go back to our example.

Cause and Effect

A cause-and-effect analysis should also be thought of as an effect-and-cause or why, why, why? analysis, as it is a two-way street, and we all know that you have a much lower chance of being hit by a car as you cross a two-way street if you look both ways. By thinking of the analysis in both ways, you give yourself a much better chance of identifying everything you need to worry about. Say you wish to treat cancer in a patient, so you do some research and learn (only) that chemotherapy can have a positive effect. You go to your patient and say, "Chemotherapy offers you a great chance of beating this illness." Had you continued your research and worked in the opposite direction—that is, to understand the other effects of chemotherapy—you may well have offered your patient this more complete news: "Chemotherapy offers you a great chance of beating this illness but may cause severe nausea after each treatment and hair loss." The fact remains that chemotherapy can cause a reduction in the cancer; by looking at all of the (possible) effects of chemotherapy we have realized that the outcome we seek is not the only likely outcome of the treatment.

It is often much easier to understand possible effects than it is to determine causes. This is because many times outcomes, or effects, are a consequence of more than one cause. A good way to begin your attempt to determine causes is to ask "Why?" at least three times. Just reflect on any episode of the television program *CSI* you have watched—a decomposing, mutilated body is found in a pool of dry blood in the middle of the Arizona desert; just one hour later (including ads), a jealous gay brother-in-law is convicted of murder, thanks to a tire track in the desert and a single hair found . . . somewhere. It turns out that it is not the apparent gunshot to the chest that caused death, but the combination of asthma, dehydration, and a snake bite! The enterprise risk management officer needs to be very concerned with the tangle of causes. Let us apply the why, why, why? approach to a more relevant example. Imagine you work for an airline that has aimed to increase profit on flights between Australia and several Asian destinations. After six months, you observe that profit is actually decreasing. To get the strategy back on track, you have to determine the cause of the erosion in profit. You seek the answer to the question "Why is profit decreasing?" and you find that it is because revenue has fallen while expenses remain the same. So you ask "Why has revenue fallen?" and you find that the marketing director decided to reduce fares to countries impacted by the 2005 tsunami, and the impact of the fare reduction exceeds the impact of higher volumes. So you ask "Why did the marketing director reduce fares to this level?" and you find that her bonus is based on volumes and she needed to increase volumes by 20% to achieve her (personal) target.

To ensure the greatest chance of achieving multiple strategic objectives, the enterprise risk management framework needs to understand and handle relationships between the myriad causes. To this end, the framework must include a formal analysis of these relationships. A common and very sensible approach is to represent causes and effects diagrammatically. Such a picture is often referred to as a strategy map and may look something like Exhibit 6.1.

One of the concerns I have with strategy maps is that a lot of people spend too much time on them. There is no limit to the number of ways the strategy map can be presented, and a person can get lost when thinking of

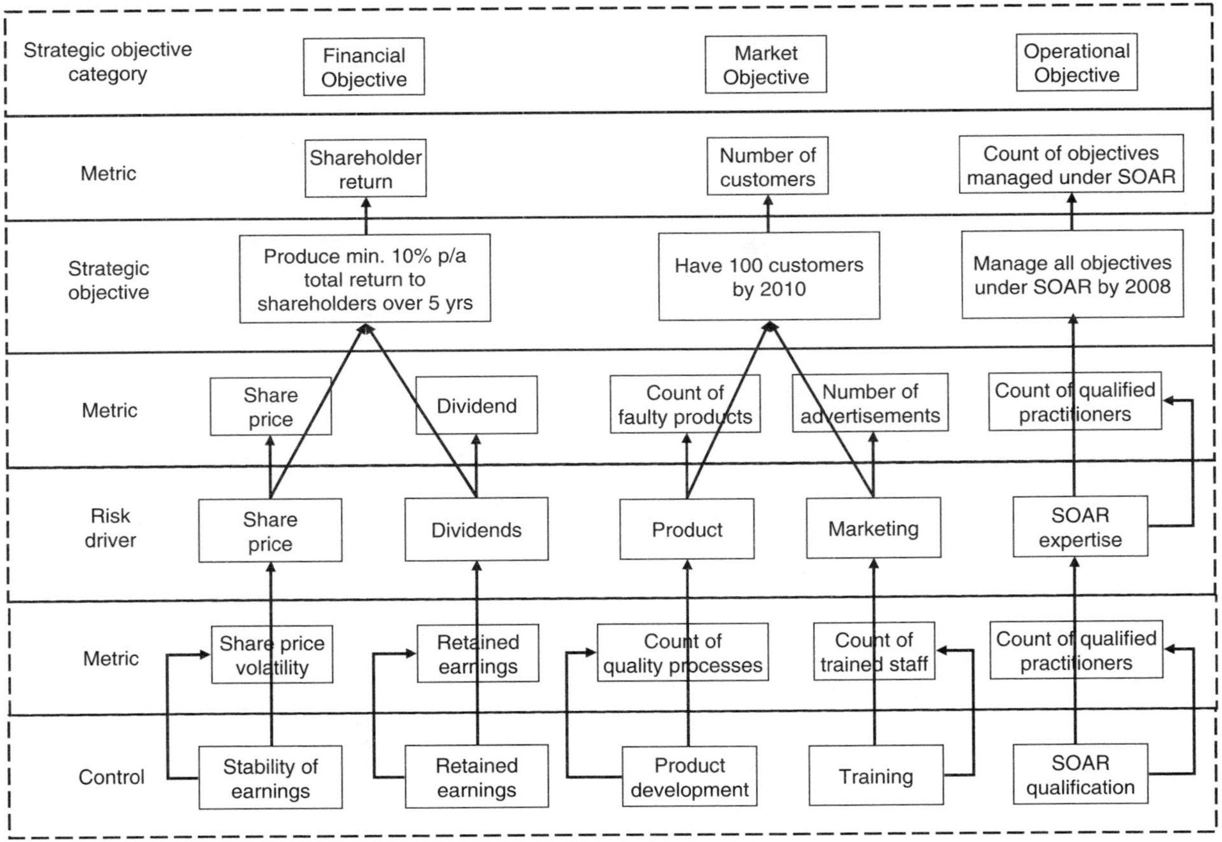

EXHIBIT 6.1 STRATEGY MAP

how best to represent the web of objectives, metrics, risks, and controls. I consider strategy maps essential visual aids, and I consider it equally important that such maps be created without *too much* thought. I am not sure how to define "too much," other than to suggest that you keep in mind that the map is just one tool you will use and you have a big job to complete; do not let the time you spend building the strategy map be disproportionate to the function it will serve. Keep in mind that most people will take a casual glance at the strategy map and say "Aha." A search for images on Google using the phrase "strategy map" returns over 1 million results—you could spend more than a lifetime just browsing images of maps created by others.

Just one more thing about the strategy map. It should be a living object, not a picture on a page as it is presented in Exhibit 6.1. Ideally, the enterprise risk manager should be able to extract data from (behind) the strategy map. Imagine if, while viewing the map in Exhibit 6.1 as, say, an .html page on your intranet, you could click on the box representing the metric "Shareholder return" and see past, present, and predicted future values of the metric. How powerful would that be? If you can do that, then you are really starting to bring the strategy and the management of the strategic objective to life. That surely must be one of the goals of the enterprise risk management office. The primary goal, of course, is to increase the likelihood of achieving strategic objectives.

Back to cause and effect and why, why, why? analysis. Do not be constrained to thinking that the latter analysis need only pose "Why?" questions. When determining metrics for strategic objectives, you can also ask "How?" and "What?" Examples might be "How are we going to achieve this objective?" and/or "What influences the outcome of this objective?" Let us try one of these questions on our greenhouse gases example. In this case, I recommend starting with "What?": "What produces greenhouse emissions?" Research will quickly reveal that coal-burning electricity plants make an enormous contribution to greenhouse gases. Without any further investigation, we might propose reducing the use of coal-burning electricity plants in order to achieve our objective of a reduction in the emission of greenhouse gases. Let us continue down the greenhouse path and ask: "How are we going to achieve this objective?" Well, the answer to our "What?" question tells us that the "How" may have something to do with reducing reliance on coal-burning electricity plants. For the purpose of this example, we will run with that and answer the "How?" question by saying "We will strive to achieve our objective of reducing the emission of greenhouse gases by reducing our use of coal-burning stations by 25%." Before we proceed to ask "Why?" we should check our current position. By asking "What?" we determined that coal-burning plants have an enormous impact on greenhouse gas emission levels. By asking "How?" we determined that we could reduce greenhouse gas emission levels by reducing our reliance on coal-burning plants. Next, we should proceed to think about appropriate metrics. Well, in this example, it is a no-brainer: One metric must be the volume of electricity produced by coal-burning generation plants. Let us now validate that metric by asking "Why would we measure the level of production of coal-burning electricity generation plants?" I could, of course, answer that question for you, but I will not. If you cannot answer it, you need to reread this section until you can. If you have read this section more than three times and still cannot answer the question, I would like you to close the book and either put it back on the shelf or give it to your 2IC.

Some readers may find the next statement redundant. For each metric, you must specify the unit of measure. Say no more. Well, except to say that some units of measure are more relevant than others.

Some tools you might like to apply to assist in setting metrics follow. Rather than telling you what they are or what they do, which is information you can get from probably tens of thousands of Web sites, I will focus on their application to setting metrics.

Cause-and-Effect Diagrams

We already have discussed cause-and-effect analysis, so there is no need to go over old ground. The diagram is just a visual representation of—you can see it coming, right?—causes and effects. It is useful in the application of the SOAR process because it provides a view on the relationships between metrics. I mean, if you have identified something as either a cause or an effect, you will have attached a metric to it, so you will be able to see the relationships between the metrics.

Causal Loop Diagrams

Causal loop diagrams help users visualize the nature of the impact of a cause; that is, does it make a positive or a negative contribution toward our objective? Generally, we set risk driver metrics for causes that make a neg-ative (or opposite) contribution to the desired outcome and control met-rics to causes that make a positive (or same) contribution. You might find an inclination to focus on the "reinforcing" loops (those that make a pos-itive contribution), as these represent progress (for want of a better term). I advise against this bias. While it is the engine that gets the car where you want it to go, you should keep the windshield wipers in good repair in case it rains.

Process Flow Charts

I have to admit, I despise process flow charts. To me, they reek of bureauc-racy, and I shudder at the thought of dusty, outdated manuals piled in office corners or, even worse, filed in a cabinet in the basement. They do, how-ever, serve as a useful reference that can help you identify points of possible failure and therefore set risk driver and control metrics. So if your strategic objective relates to something for which a process flow diagram exists, take a look at it. Imagine your strategic objective is to manage the risks associ-ated with strategic plans according to the SOAR methodology. If you are trying to set risk and control metrics, you could use the SOAR process flow diagram as a reference. (See Exhibit 6.2.)

With little effort, we can set a number of risk driver metrics, such as:

- The number of strategic objectives for which metrics have not been defined
- The number of times metric values have not been observed

We can also set some control metrics, including:

- The number of reviews of cause-and-effect analysis
- The degree of *correlation* between risk driver metrics and strategic objective metrics

I would like to spend a minute discussing correlation. Think of correla-tion as the degree to which two metrics are related or, if you like, the strength of the relationship between two metrics. An example of the use of the term "correlation" is: There is a high correlation between sales of um-brellas and rainfall. This sentence means that the relationship between sales

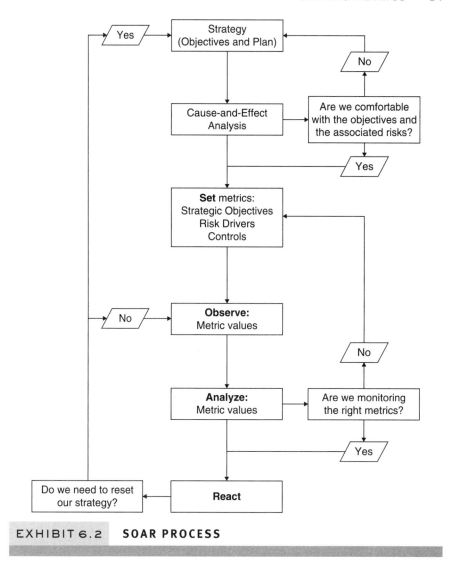

EXHIBIT 6.2   SOAR PROCESS

and rainfall is strong. With reference to our greenhouse gases example, we could say that there is a high correlation between the volume of electricity produced by coal-burning generation plants and damage to the ozone layer. The measurement of correlation between risk driver metrics and strategic objective metrics (and also between control metrics and strategic objective metrics) is an important aspect of the SOAR process. Measurement of correlation is performed in step 3, analyze, of the process and helps answer the question: Are we monitoring the right metrics? We discuss this again in Chapter 8.

Regression Analysis

Although I believe that the application of regression analysis to setting metrics is limited, I think it at least worth a mention. For some strategic objectives, you may have sufficient data on both the strategic objective metric and the risk driver/control metrics to make regression analysis worthwhile. Very simply stated, regression analysis is about the determination of the relationships between causes and outcomes. In this regard, it has some similarity to correlation (i.e., they both involve the examination of the relationships between variables). Correlation is limited to the measurement of the relationship between two variables, while regression analysis can handle more than one explanatory variable and can describe the relationship between variables in greater detail. I do not think it is worth spending too much time on regression analysis here. Suffice it to say that it may be valuable in helping you discover/validate risk driver/control metrics. If you have adequate historical data, get your analyst to give it a shot.

Sensitivity Analysis

Similar to regression analysis, sensitivity analysis requires a bit of data. If you have the data available, I highly recommend that you apply sensitivity analysis to help you determine where your focus should lie. Basically, sensitivity analysis helps you determine the relative importance of your risk driver and control metrics (i.e., it reveals the degree of influence each risk driver/control metric has on the strategic objective metric). This very simple example can illustrate. Imagine we have this function to describe a strategic objective metric:

$$SOM = X - 2 \times Y$$

A movement of 1 in X is going to cause a movement of 1 in SOM. A movement of 1 in Y is going to cause a movement of -2 in SOM. SOM is twice as sensitive to movements in Y as it is to movements in X. You get two things out of sensitivity analysis: From the model that describes the strategic objective metric, you get some very good indication of risk driver/control metrics, and from the analysis itself, you get an appreciation of the relative importance of the risk driver/control metrics that you can use to ensure appropriate assignment of resource.

If, for example, you are a retailer of watches and you have a truckload of historical data available, you might be able to determine how sensitive sales volumes are to all of the different variables: price (seems like a pretty obvious one), time of year, dollars spent on marketing, and so on. By observing how one variable (e.g., sales volume) relates to another (e.g., price), you can easily determine risk and control metrics. If your analysis reveals that dollars spent on marketing have twice the impact of adjusting the price, you would concentrate on marketing.

Scenario Analysis

Sometimes referred to as what–if analysis, scenario analysis employs expert judgment to determine a range of risk scenarios and their outcomes. It is employed to help you gain an understanding of possible outcomes should certain events transpire. The experts are responsible for defining the scenarios: the things that may happen (leading to an event) or the events that may transpire. Exhibit 6.3, first presented in Chapter 1, shows the "flow" of risk in the risk universe.

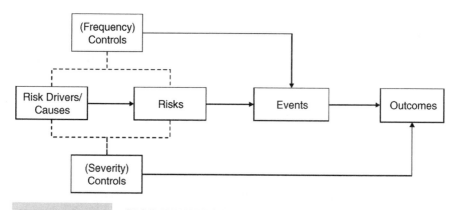

EXHIBIT 6.3   RISK UNIVERSE

In scenario analysis, we are considering what might happen along the path to an outcome. We can jump in at any point, from possible values of metrics for risk drivers and controls, through possible events to possible outcomes. Scenario analysis typically is conducted in a workshop. As I said, scenario analysis usually is based on expert judgment, so the workshop brings the experts together to . . . think! Ideally, the experts are trying to imagine scenarios relating to new points on the distribution of possible outcomes.

Remember that what we are striving to understand is the distribution of possible outcomes, where the outcome of most interest is the future value of our strategic objective metric. We want to be able to *visualize risk* through the probability distribution, which might look like Exhibit 6.4.

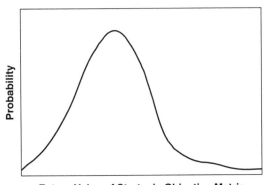

Future Value of Strategic Objective Metric

EXHIBIT 6.4 **PROBABILITY DISTRIBUTION AS A VISUALIZATION OF RISK**

Of course, some values on the axes are required, but not for our current purpose. With in mind the aim of plotting outcomes, the job of the workshop participants comes down to generating a set of pairs of numbers. Each pair of numbers comprises a future metric value and a probability. The output of the scenario analysis might be something as easy as a table containing a description of the scenario, a probability *estimate* and a metric value *estimate*. Exhibit 6.5 is an example.

By the way, do not spend any time considering the validity of the numbers in Exhibit 6.5; it is just an example of how the results of the scenario analysis might be presented.

EXHIBIT 6.5   EXAMPLE RECORD OF SCENARIO ANALYSIS

Description of Scenario	Probability that Scenario Will Occur	Metric Value if Scenario Occurs
Global increase in demand for electricity of 15%	5%	3
Lack of acceptance of nuclear power plants as a substitute for coal-burning power stations	10%	2
Broad public acceptance of the contribution of coal-burning power stations to global warming	2%	7

If you spend one or two minutes considering the example outputs in Exhibit 6.5, you might realize a couple of things and raise a couple of questions. Your realizations/questions might include:

- How do the experts determine the probability?
- How do they determine the metric value?
- There could be thousands of possible outcomes.
- Those numbers might be hard to validate; should we really rely on them?

Good questions! A fair and common criticism of scenario analysis is that it is often hard to substantiate. For our purpose, though, that does not really matter. We are using scenario analysis as a tool to help identify metrics relating to strategic objectives. We may or may not use the probability and outcome estimates generated by the experts, but we will use the scenario descriptions—they might imply a metric we had not thought of.

Let me take a moment to explain why "estimate" appears in italics in my earlier statement that the output of the scenario analysis might be something as easy as a table containing a description of the scenario, a probability *estimate* and a metric value *estimate*. It is to remind you that the numbers we are producing are . . . estimates, not, for example, historical observations.

EXAMPLES OF METRICS

Exhibits 6.6, 6.7, and 6.8 are a few examples of useful metrics for each of the objective classes.

EXHIBIT 6.6	EXAMPLE METRICS RELATING TO FINANCIAL OBJECTIVES

Objective	Metric Class	Metric
Growth in sales	Objective	Monthly/annual sales
	Risk driver	Number of active sales opportunities/orders
	Control	Percent of salespeople who have attended the sales training course

EXHIBIT 6.7	EXAMPLE METRICS RELATING TO MARKET OBJECTIVES

Objective	Metric Class	Metric
To be ranked number 1	Objective	Rank according to some survey
	Risk driver	Results of minisurveys
	Control	Count of customer complaints

EXHIBIT 6.8	EXAMPLE METRICS RELATING TO OPERATIONAL OBJECTIVES

Objective	Metric Class	Metric
Reduce operational error	Objective	Error rate (e.g., count of erroneous transactions/total number of transactions)
	Risk driver	Number of transactions performed per person
	Control	Percent of staff performing transactions who have attended the transaction processing training course

SETTING TARGET VALUES FOR METRICS

Determining a (single) target value for each metric for each strategic objective (i.e., for all metrics within the strategic objective class) is paramount to successful execution of the SOAR process. In effect, attaining the target value of the metric becomes your objective, as the enterprise risk management officer. If the target value is correctly determined, reaching the target value is the same as achieving the strategic objective. So it is very important to determine the target value of the strategic objective metric correctly.

Sometimes this is a very straightforward exercise; usually this is the case for financial objectives. It becomes harder to determine target metric values when you incorporate the notion of desirability discussed earlier. Take the case where your objective is to be spoken of favorably in the press. What should the target value for your metric be: 5? 50? 500? 22? The answer, of course, is that it does not matter what value you set as the target for the metric. What is important is that you put in place a sensible system of measurement, including a measurement scale, for the metric and that the target value makes sense under that system.

The concept of scale is an important one to address. If you are measuring the distance between two cities, you would probably choose miles or kilometers as your unit of measure, although there are a number of other reasonable choices and hundreds of unreasonable ones. Another reasonable choice might by flight time. An unreasonable choice would be pillows. It is possible to measure the distance between two cities by the number of pillows that could be placed end to end between the two places, but that is a pretty silly way to do it. So we should discuss scales and systems of measurement in a little more detail, and now is as good a time as any.

Generally, choosing a system of measurement, including a measurement scale, is a subjective exercise. In some cases, your choice set may be limited and obvious, but this will not always be the case. If your objective relates to air quality, for example, you might choose to refer to ISO (International Organization for Standardization) 4226:1993 Air Quality—General Aspects—Units of Measurement. You might wish to refer to that if you are having trouble sleeping too. It is difficult to imagine a case where only one system of measurement is possible. Even in those cases where it seems pretty clear what system should be applied, it is probably quite easy to suggest a reasonable alternative. Let us say your objective is to achieve sales of CAD500 million. This one seems pretty straightforward: Your system of measurement should have a lot to do with the (accounting) system you use for the capture of sales information. But CAD500 million might represent 50 million units (at CAD10 each). Or it might represent an increase of 10% on last year. The point is that there are a number of suitable metrics and measurement systems. Even if we agree that the metric will relate to the objective of CAD500 million (as opposed to, say, units or percentage increase), what should the target metric value be: 500? Seems reasonable. But it could just as well be 50, and the system of measurement could employ some function like "sales in CAD divided by 10" to calculate the metric value.

Some points to consider when choosing a system of measurement for your metrics follow.

- Keep it as simple as possible, both conceptually and computationally. In our example, we could have set the metric value to be equal to the natural log of the square root of sales if we had really wanted to. But what is the point in that? If you make it complex, you are just going to have to spend time explaining it to someone. Once you have come up with the measurement system, imagine trying to answer this question posed by a senior manager: "Why do you measure it that way?"

- Make sure it is intuitive. If you are a Canadian company that measures sales in CAD and you have an objective to achieve sales of CAD500 million, Canadian dollars seems like a reasonable choice for your unit of measure. You could choose euros, if you like, and convert the CAD sales information from your accounting system to euros each reporting period, but that would be a strange thing to do.

- Make sure the scale is appropriately granular. Although it is possible to measure the thickness of a human hair in kilometers, that would be a very strange choice of unit of measure. You really want a system where the value can be expressed in whole units, or possibly one level below that, to one decimal place, for example. To say that a strand of wool is 0.000000000000016 kilometers thick is not really helpful, but to say that a typical strand is 16 microns thick and ranges from 5 to 25 microns is more enlightening, even if you (like me) do not know what a micron is.

- Try to keep any requisite mathematical manipulation as simple as possible. Simple functions, such as multiply and divide, are commonly understood (even among those in senior management), but do not try anything much more tricky.

- Where possible, employ a commonly accepted system without changing it. If you are a Canadian company that measures sales in CAD and you have an objective to achieve sales of CAD500 million,

Canadian dollars seems like a reasonable choice for your unit of measure, and you may as well apply the *system* that goes with it: that 2 is bigger than 1, for example, and that it operates in base 10. Having said that, I would love to see someone try to explain that a system of measurement for a metric is similar to that used for Canadian dollars, except that it is in base 9.

Unlike strategic objective metrics, control and risk driver metrics do not require target values. This is not to say that they *should* not have target values; indeed, in some cases, setting target values for control metrics is a very good idea. You probably will find you need to exercise a little more lateral thinking when determining measurement systems for control and risk driver metrics than is required for strategic objective metrics (particularly strategic objective metrics for financial objectives). This is due to the fact that many controls and drivers do not really have popular metrics. Let us take the case of an aircraft early warning system, a device found in aircraft that gives early warning of a possible midair collision with another aircraft. It is a control. Or is it? I sometimes get confused between risk drivers and controls. I mean, this one strikes me as a control, because it is referred to as an early warning system and it is intended to give warning of a possible collision, but then I think about it as just the device for recording and reporting the values of a risk driver metric. The risk driver metric is the distance between the two aircraft. The device has predefined triggers that alert you when the risk driver metric hits a certain level (i.e., the distance between the two aircraft becomes too small). But it is a control, for sure; it is something that has been put in place to reduce the possibility of an event. Up in the air, the pilot probably has a light on the dashboard that indicates whether the system is active or not. That light is a control. So should the metric for this control be something that can take just two values representing either "active" or "inactive"? Seems reasonable to me.

Let us try something else. Imagine your strategic objective is to be rated number one in customer service and a control you have in place is the provision of customer service training to all customer-facing staff. What should your metric be, and what should the measurement system look like? Well, let us agree (or agree to disagree; it is up to you) on the metric first. As will quite often be the case, there are a number of reasonable options (and thousands of absurd ones). I am going to suggest that the metric be the average score received in the customer service training final exam. (If you like, take a few minutes to consider options and even different ways of calculating the average.) Having selected the metric, the choice of measurement system is really quite straightforward; just use the results from the exams. The only question, really, is one of expression; do you maintain the percentage format applied to the exam results, or do you take absolute values? Here is one way to resolve that dilemma: Ask yourself "Who cares?" If the answer is "no one" (or "no one worth worrying about"), then flip a coin.

By now you should be getting some notion of one of my underlying doctrine, but I will articulate it here just in case. There is no need to strive for perfection in order to implement the SOAR methodology successfully. Just like a recipe, the methodology prescribes steps, ingredients, and measures, but you do not have to be precise when following the recipe; think of it as a guide. The more expert you become in the SOAR methodology, the less you need to refer to the recipe. We are all a bit different, and the world would be no fun if we were all the same. Add a pinch of salt if you like, or put the milk in *before* the egg. Go on, I *dare* you. I'd rather you think about the fact that you have guests arriving who expect to eat before midnight than worry about whether the teaspoon you have just grabbed from the drawer is a standard size. Does it look more like a teaspoon than a tablespoon? Fine, it will do. I am confident that if you apply the SOAR methodology in a disciplined fashion, you will help your organization be more successful in attaining its strategic objectives.

Despite all of the references to cooking, I offer this advice for the execution of the SOAR methodology: Do not make a meal of it. If you need to define a metric, just consider a few options and choose one within a reasonable time frame. If you need to choose a system of measurement, just consider a few options and choose one within a reasonable time frame.

We are nearing the end of the set step of the SOAR process, so I would just like to note the key points about setting metrics:

- A strategic objective is represented by a single strategic objective metric under the SOAR process.

- For each strategic objective, you should attempt to define a risk driver metric and a control indicator metric in addition to the strategic objective metric.

- A metric has a unit of measurement and a measurement scale associated with it.

- You must define a target value for the strategic objective metric.

- It may be valuable to define trigger values for risk driver and control metrics.

CHAPTER 7

Observe Metric Values

In this chapter we discuss the observation of metric values. For some metrics, including those that relate to common units of measure, such as money, time, percent, and so on, observation can be quite straightforward, assuming remarkably common little things like computer systems do not get in the way. Others are going to be somewhat more tricky and may require the application of yet more imagination. With regard to metrics, you must adhere to Galileo's principle in order to apply the SOAR methodology. I would argue that you must apply this concept for the successful management of strategic objectives, whether you apply the SOAR methodology or not:

> *Measure all that can be measured and render measurable all that defies measurement.*

I hope you are now familiar with the quote.

I am going to generalize my previous statement and say that you should apply the concept of making things measurable when you are managing anything.

OBSERVATION METHODS

There are dozens of ways to gather data. I will explore but a handful of the most common methods of observing metric values here.

Gathering Available Data

Some data for the metrics you wish to record will be readily available, as perhaps they were captured for some other purpose. Examples might include staff training records, annual leave data, and sales data. Although likely not in the form you want them, they are lurking around in some database (possibly that data dump, the enterprise data warehouse) somewhere in the organization. Whether it is worth trying to find the information, extract it, and correct it rather than just capture it again is up to you to determine.

According to a 2003 study by the School of Information Management and Systems at the University of California at Berkeley called "How Much Information?" the amount of new information stored on various media doubled in the three years to 2002. I have doubt whether the additional information stored throughout that period was in fact new. I am far more inclined to believe that the vast majority was merely a copy of preexisting information. Thus, the growth in information is due not to new information but to duplication, triplication, and so on. I guess the term "new" includes new instances of something that already existed. Just think of some amusing .jpg file you have received from a friend and saved to your C drive or perhaps to a local area network and shared with others. How many copies of that do you think now exist? Or how many times have you struggled to find a file diligently filed within the past few months and, on finally locating it, decided to save it to one or two other locations to make it easier to find next time? Or what about compressed files (e.g., .zip), where you keep both the compressed and uncompressed formats? How often do you go through your files and delete the old stuff you are never going to use again? Never, right? Well, maybe from time to time you have to: say, when you try to do something on your computer and you run out of disk space. Or you try to send an email but you get a message telling you your mailbox is full. Then you do one of two things: You get your computer to archive anything older than 90 days, or you sort by size and delete the 10 biggest files. The rest remains—to be included in the University of California's next survey, no doubt!

The university's study does not address the quality of data, something I am almost certain would be of great interest to research. I believe that the proportion of data that contains material error is high. Another prejudice leads me to believe that the vast majority of the data held is absolutely useless. Throughout my working life, I have seen far too many examples of how data is captured, manipulated, misrepresented, and corrupted to have any faith in it unless the data has been exhaustively checked and cleansed.

Many of the problems with data exist before someone interprets—or, more likely—misinterprets the data. Maybe you have a problem capturing the data, or finding the data dictionary for some database that was conceived six years ago, never properly documented, and intended for some other department. Or maybe you know the data is sitting there but it will take your information technology guys six months to write a program that will create a flat file for you. Then when they deliver the file to you, you realize they have misinterpreted what you said when you asked for "daily sales, expressed in EUR, by store location." Only a database administrator could misinterpret that.

Without any sort of analysis whatsoever, but based on years of frustration caused by having to wrestle with data, I estimate that the volume of useful, accurate data increases at a very slow, steady rate. Accordingly, the volume of useful, accurate data as a proportion of the total volume of data diminishes rapidly.

Something that is even more frightening is the volume of data that never gets recorded. How many times have you interacted with an organization and been 100% satisfied by the experience? It is not common, right? On how many occasions has the organization recorded your dissatisfaction? That is not common either, is it? There is a huge volume of incredibly valuable data that never gets recorded (so that it can later be damaged and misunderstood). Just think of how many times you have gone to purchase a particular item from a store, and none of that particular item is on the shelf, so you walk out. The fact that the store could have sold one more unit of that item is not captured. Imagine now that you are the person responsible for ensuring that the strategic objective "to grow sales by 10%" is met. Would that information be incredibly valuable? Imagine knowing that if an extra unit had been on the shelf, it would have been sold!

As far as the SOAR process is concerned, you *can* have *too much* data. You will likely accumulate too much data when you have mistakenly determined too high a frequency for collection of metric values or when you have set too many metrics. I would not worry about that too much; you are not likely to be collecting megabytes of data, so 50% more than is necessary is not going to bring your organization's database, nor the database administrator, to its (or his or her) knees. Of course, you want to avoid passing useless data on to anyone; you should identify that it is useless, somehow address that fact, and continue working with the useful stuff.

In order to determine whether the data is useful or not, examine the correlation between the metric values you have observed and the strategic objective metric. If the correlation between the values (i.e., that of the risk driver/control metric and the strategic objective metric) is low, there is little point observing that metric. In this case, analyze how you set that metric to determine whether some improvement can be made in this area.

Calculating Data

From gathered data, you can calculate additional data. For example, you may gather data every time an operational error occurs: who was responsible, what they were doing, how the mistake was made, the impact, and so on. A simple value you might calculate is the count of operational errors over a period. The list of useful calculated values includes (without exclusion) count, sum, average, standard deviation, minimum, and maximum.

Calculating summary statistics is often a good idea when the frequency of observation is high (say, daily) and short-term movements are quite volatile but there is a stable long-term trend. If your objective is to reduce volatility of earnings (and remember, I am deliberately lazy in the statement of the strategic objective), analysis of daily revenue might be onerous and misleading.

Self-Assessment

When metric values are not readily available, self-assessment *can* be an excellent way to determine them. Self-assessment is very often applied to risk and control indicators and is almost always a three-step process. Let us take control self-assessment (as it is currently performed, i.e., outside the SOAR process) as an example. Control self-assessment is a popular element of operational risk management frameworks. In the first step, the owner of the control (or "control metric" in SOAR terminology) completes a questionnaire designed to measure the effectiveness of the control or the level of (inherent) risk. In the second step, an independent party validates the responses of the control (or metric) owner. The measured value of the control is the indicator. (In SOAR terminology, the last sentence would read: The measured value of the metric is the metric value.) Some time later—the time frame depends on the frequency of collection of relevant data—

the third step consists of an analysis of related outcomes to (further) validate the assessment.

Let us use the example of "strengthening our brand" as the strategic objective. The enterprise risk management office has observed that negative publicity adversely impacts brand strength and should be avoided. The "control" that is put in place is a policy to be adhered to by all employees of "not speaking badly of the organization." After the policy is put in place, the self-assessment is conducted. As a result, the distribution of assessment results is redrawn. Imagine, though, that the questionnaire was ill-conceived and failed to recognize how widely the policy had been distributed and how well employees were adhering to it. For example, the questionnaire might ask you to rate the quality of the public relations policy, choosing from these responses: very poor, poor, OK, good, and very good. The questionnaire might fail to ask you to state the percentage of employees who have attended the public relations workshop during the assessment period and fail to prompt you to select from an appropriate set of responses, such as less than 10%, 10–25%, 25–75%, 75–90%, or greater than 90%. Sure enough, one of the people among the 75 to 90% who have *not* attended the workshop opens his mouth to a reporter, resulting in negative publicity and proving the policy to be worth only the paper that it was written on. The example highlights a couple of issues: (1) Assessments must be validated by correlating assessment results with observable outcomes, and (2) assessment questionnaires must be well designed.

As a rule of thumb, you probably will find that values of metrics for strategic objectives are calculated, values of metrics for risk drivers are gathered, and values of metrics for controls are obtained via self-assessment.

RECORDING OBSERVATIONS OF METRICS

Each observed value of a metric should be recorded to allow analysis. At the time the metric value is observed and recorded, some process should be in place to ensure the integrity of the record.

Now let us think of a strategic objective that may appear to be difficult to assign one or more metrics to. We can make it easy for ourselves by picking some ridiculous objective, such as: We want our customers to love us. To measure our achievement of this objective, we need to measure the level or quantity of love our customers have for us. And as anyone who has enjoyed a relationship would know, there is no unit of measure for love. Well, there are diamonds, but that is it. So we must define the "love metric." There you go; we have defined the metric to be applied to this objective: the love metric. Now all we have to do is observe its current value. How do we do that? By surveying our customers via a questionnaire that poses questions that enable us to quantify their love for us. Examples of such questions might be:

- How much do you enjoy interacting with our organization?
- How often do you recommend our organization to your friends?
- How strongly do you recommend our organization to your friends?

The beauty of the survey/questionnaire approach is that you can restrict the range of responses participants can give. This is an important element for reliable measurement of metrics. Possible answers to the example questions could be:

- I really enjoy it; I hate it; I don't care.
- Every waking moment; never; sometimes.
- Very strongly; I don't; whatever.

Behind the scenes, the SOAR methodology applies a score to each response. For question 1, the answers might be scored 3, 1, and 2, respectively. The higher the score, the greater the love. Furthermore, the SOAR methodology applies weights to each of the questions. You might judge question 1 to be less indicative of love than the other two and so assign a weight of 0.8 to question 1 and weight the other two questions at 0.1. You can see that there is some science and art behind determining all of the elements mentioned here: the questions, the answers, the answer scores, and the weights.

FREQUENCY OF OBSERVATION

Just a moment ago we conceived and considered the love metric. As its value is measured via survey, likely we could not measure such a metric any more frequently than annually. Every metric will have a natural limit to the frequency with which data can be collected. In determining the frequency of data collection for any metric, you need to answer these questions:

- What is the greatest frequency of collection possible?
- How frequently does the measured value demonstrate a material change?
- If I collect data at anything less than the maximum possible frequency, what is the chance that I miss something important?
- How much data can I actually work with?

Consider for a moment a retailer that uses sales as a metric for some objective. The retailer probably has the ability to monitor sales in an almost real time or continuous manner, but is that necessary? Almost certainly it is not.

TRIGGERS

Triggers can be very useful particularly, though not exclusively, for metrics for which frequency of collection is high. When used correctly, triggers allow you to take your eye off the ball for a moment. Triggers are values of the metric that you have determined are worthy of note when they are observed. Closely associated with triggers are the concepts of materiality and tolerance, which both relate to how comfortable we feel when movements in metric values are relatively small. Triggers are set at the boundaries of that comfort level.

Like much of what this book discusses, triggers are a concept we apply in everyday life. Consider, for example, your decision process when you have your nearly dry wash hanging on the clothesline and you decide to go out. If it is sunny, you do not give the wash a second thought. If there are dark clouds above, you might decide to bring the wash in. The lazy ones among us might wait for the first drop of rain before making the mad dash to the backyard, basket in hand.

Exhibit 7.1 shows observed values that breach the triggers on three occasions (in periods 3, 4, and 7). The enterprise risk management office should have predefined actions for these occasions. Trigger levels are typically set some distance away from the forecast. Recall that a forecast value is really a distribution of values. In the exhibit (and in most exhibits in this

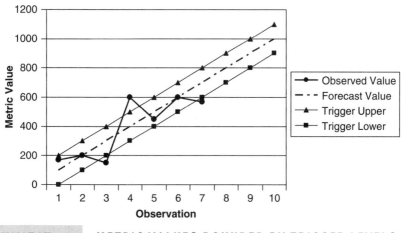

EXHIBIT 7.1   METRIC VALUES BOUNDED BY TRIGGER LEVELS

book), the forecast value at each observation point is one point from the distribution of possible values. The point chosen to display on the graph is typically either the most likely value (i.e., that with the highest probability, the mode) or the average value (the mean). Triggers remind us, and are a function of the fact, that there is a distribution of possible outcomes at each point. I discuss this again a little later.

Before we proceed to the analyze step of the SOAR process, here is a reminder of what we have discussed in relation to observation:

- There are myriad ways to collect observations of metric values, including gathering existing data, calculating data, and self-assessment.
- Observations should be recorded in a reliable and convenient manner. When I say "convenient," I mean easy to both store and use.
- You need to determine an appropriate observation frequency. The frequency needs to be often enough to observe all material movements and not so often as to create noise.
- Triggers are a valuable tool that will help you identify potentially troublesome metric values.

CHAPTER 8

Analyze Movements in Metrics

The analyze step in the SOAR process is, like most things in life, conceptually very simple. It involves the examination of the observed values with a view to understanding the implications for future values of the metrics. You can break the step into two parts: (1) conducting the analysis and (2) presenting it.

CONDUCTING THE ANALYSIS

There is no magic in conducting the analysis: Simply monitor the change in value of the metric over time. Your analysis can be as sophisticated or as simple as you like, subject to the volume of data you collect for the metric. Imagine the love metric defined in Chapter 7. It is not a metric that you are likely to get a value for every day; you would be more likely to conduct the survey on an annual basis, I guess. Compare that to the metric attached to another example objective, namely: We want to increase daily revenue to CAD10 million by end 2010. It is quite easy to define the appropriate metric; it is daily revenue, right? With adequate systems in place, you would be able to record daily revenue every day. (With slightly less adequate systems, you might be able to get daily revenue at the end of each month, or you might be able to get monthly revenue at the end of each month and from that estimate daily revenue numbers.) Remember Galileo's words:

> *Measure all that can be measured and render measurable all that defies measurement.*

After two years, we might have two observations for the love metric and a few hundred observations for daily revenue. Without being a statistician

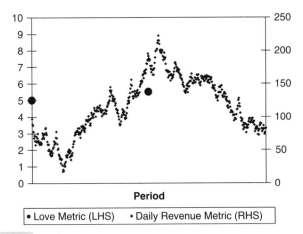

EXHIBIT 8.1   GRAPH OF TWO METRICS WITH DIFFERENT OBSERVATION FREQUENCIES

and based on our earlier discussion of distributions, we can imagine that we could achieve a higher level of sophistication in the analysis of the daily revenue metric than the love metric. Exhibit 8.1 provides views of the two metrics.

Imagine that you now have to analyze the two metrics further in order to forecast future values. Without too much effort, you can add a trend line for each number series. It might look something like Exhibit 8.2.

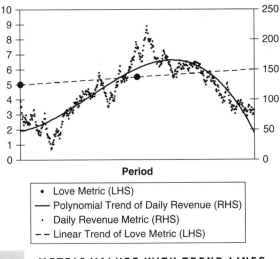

EXHIBIT 8.2   METRIC VALUES WITH TREND LINES

Enterprise risk managers should be able to understand the relative virtues of the two trend lines. The trend line for the daily revenue metric has some statistical basis. However, there is very little—probably too little—information to support the trend line for the love metric. What can you do in this case? Well, consider the way the love metric was calculated; it was measured as the average value of survey results. As mentioned, likely it would not be practical to conduct the survey more often than annually. What if we can conduct minisurveys every month? Imagine the annual survey includes 1,000 respondents. Why not conduct a monthly survey of, say, 100 people? You might then get something like Exhibit 8.3.

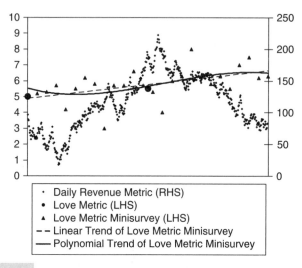

EXHIBIT 8.3   **INCREASING OBSERVATION FREQUENCY**

In Exhibit 8.3, we have about 20 observations for the love metric—probably sufficient to have some confidence in the trend line. When analyzing the love metric, we must take into consideration the fact that the measurements from the minisurveys are likely to boast different characteristics from the annual survey, for at least two reasons. The minisurveys include only 100 responses, so extreme survey scores are likely to have a more significant impact on the average. The minisurveys may include some "recent event" bias. For example, the observation of the love metric (based on a minisurvey) with a value around 3 might be because the organization did something wrong and suffered some bad publicity. This publicity was fresh on the minds of survey participants, so the average score was relatively low. Imagine if that really was the case—that the survey results were significantly impacted by such an event. As the enterprise risk manager, that would be great news, wouldn't it? Now what you have to do is make sure you get good publicity just before the next annual survey!

In Exhibit 8.3 I have added two trend lines for the value of the love metric based on minisurvey results. This is to highlight the importance of having someone with strong analytical and statistical skills on your team. The analyst should be able to justify the selection of one or more analysis methods. This person should be able to explain why he or she believes a straight-line interpolation is more or less appropriate than, say, a logarithmic interpolation. As the enterprise risk manager, you should recognize that different approaches are available and that some will be more appropriate than others. You should know what questions to ask of your analyst.

Now let us get back to the discussion of the trend lines. The dashed, gently upward-sloping line gives the impression that the metric value is going to continue moving slowly but surely upward. The solid curved line gives the impression that we have reached a plateau and are now coming down a bit. So if I were to estimate the value of the love metric based on the first (dashed) trend line, I would say that the next value of the love metric based on the minisurvey is going to be a little higher than where the trend line ends, say around 6.5. If I were to estimate the next value of the love metric based on the second trend line (the curved line), I would guess it is going to be a little below where that trend line ends, say around 6.3. So I have two possible values of the love metric for the next period; *perfect!* Why is that such great news? Because we know that we do not predict a single value; we generate a distribution of possible values and, as enterprise risk managers operating under the SOAR methodology, we think and speak in terms of distributions.

In just a little while we will discuss how to generate distributions in more detail. Although we will not discuss it again, you have just seen one way to generate possible future values: Ask your software package to add trend lines to plots of observed values. The reason we do not discuss this topic again is that it lacks something. Can you guess what it lacks? Extrapolation of the future value or values of a metric from a trend line only gives you the possible future values of the metrics; it does not give you any clue regarding the probability associated with that value. We need to apply some method that allows us to estimate both the value and the probability of that value in order to draw the (probability) distribution (of the metric value). I think it is very useful to refer to the distribution as the probability distribution of the metric value. Of course, being lazy, I am going to continue to refer to it as the "distribution," but I urge you to do better. It is useful because it states exactly what we are talking about. "Distribution" does not carry much meaning. But "probability distribution of the metric value" fully describes the topic. As I said, in just a little while we will examine some methods for generating probability distributions of metric values.

VALIDATING THE DATA

An important part of analyzing data is *validating* the data. If the graph of a metric over time looks like Exhibit 8.4, you would check and double-check the most recently observed value before proceeding with the analysis.

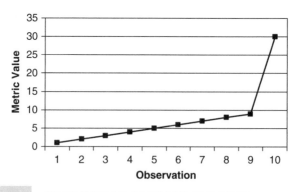

EXHIBIT 8.4   GRAPH THAT APPEARS STRANGE

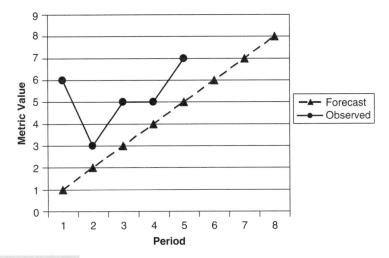

EXHIBIT 8.5   GRAPH OF FORECAST AND OBSERVED VALUES

Let us look at a more interesting example, one that we will carry through to the discussion of the react step. Imagine the plot of historical observations versus forecast values looks something like that shown in Exhibit 8.5.

The analysis of the movements in metrics should comprise five things:

1. **Validation of the observed values.** I am an advocate of the maker/checker or two-eyes approach, but even that will allow erroneous values to slip through, so the analyst must independently validate metric values.

2. **Determination of the cause(s) of volatility in the metric.** This determination includes an analysis of the correlation between values of metrics for risk drivers and for strategic objectives (to confirm that you have correctly identified the right drivers) and of the correlation between values of metrics for controls and for strategic objectives (to confirm that you have correctly identified the right controls and that they are effective).

3. **Review (and reissue) of the forecast.** Review the forecast to ensure that it was based on a reasonable estimate of the volatility of the metric and to determine whether it needs to be reissued. By "reissued" I mean create a new one. Every regular analysis will

include a new version of the forecast that takes into consideration the fact that another period has passed. At the very least, the forecast will shift by virtue of the fact that time has passed. As a consequence, a forecast value must be replaced with an observed value.

4. **Supporting documentation.** Keep this documentation as a record of steps 1 to 3.

5. **Presentation of the findings.** Presentation is discussed later in the chapter.

The supporting documentation might be structured like that shown in Exhibit 8.6.

EXHIBIT 8.6   SOAR ANALYSIS EXAMPLE

Date of analysis: DDMMYYYY

Summary of Strategic Objective
Strategic Objective: To be loved by our customers
Strategic Objective Metric: Love metric
Risk Driver Metric: Count of records of customer dissatisfaction
Control Metric: Count of staff members who have attended the how-to-make-our-customers-love-us training course (1 hour, including morning tea)

STRATEGIC OBJECTIVE METRIC VALUES (DATA)

Period	Observed Value	Forecast Value
1	6	1
2	3	2
3	5	3
4	5	4
5	7	5
6		6
7		7
8		8

STRATEGIC OBJECTIVE METRIC VALUES PLOT

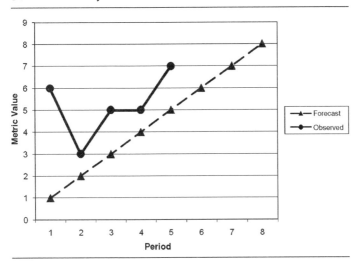

Validation of Observed Metric Values Description

I took a random sample of 100 customer surveys and checked that the score had been calculated and recorded correctly. I found the score to be more than 95% accurate in 99 cases and 90% accurate in the other case. In all cases, the score had been recorded correctly in our database. I judged the degree of error to be acceptable and assumed it would hold for the remaining surveys.

Analysis of Volatility in Metric Description

The survey was cleverly designed to include four groups of questions relating to different aspects of customer happiness. The first group of questions, for example, relates to how customers feel when they are in one of our stores. The total survey score is a weighted average of the four subscores. I examined the movement in the subscores and found that the volatility of the love metric is almost entirely due to volatility in the subscore relating to a group of questions designed to measure customer satisfaction with respect to the value they perceive we offer. Analysis of the responses to individual questions within this category revealed no discernible patterns. Responses to questions in the "value" category are best described as random. To validate this, I reweighted the four categories of questions, reducing the weight applicable to the "value" category to 0. The plot of adjusted historical values versus forecast is shown in the graph at the top of page 88.

Review of Forecast Description

I reviewed the assumptions and inputs behind the forecast, which was produced prior to the first observation of the love metric. The forecast value for the first period was based on a similar survey conducted 10 years ago, and the forecast value for the ultimate (eighth) period was based on hope—that we would achieve our target. The values for the remaining periods were simply interpolated. On the basis that the original forecast methodology was flawed and in the presence of observed values, I determined that a review of the forecast was required. The new forecast is based

(Continued)

EXHIBIT 8.6   (CONTINUED)

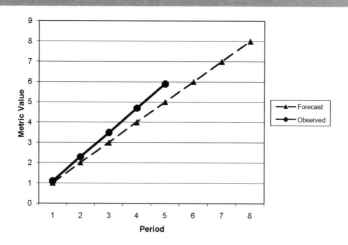

entirely on observed values and relevant external factors, such as our decision to close three stores and increase prices by an average 10% within the remaining period of the objective. In addition, the new forecast assumes that the metric be redefined to exclude the "value" score and the observed values have been adjusted to remove that factor. This is on the basis that continuing to include that random component does not help the organization reach its objective or determine whether it has reached its objective. The revised forecast and observed values appear next.

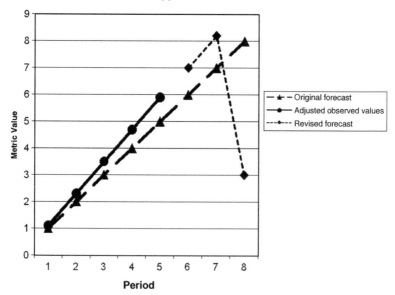

Note that the ultimate forecast value for the metric takes into consideration the anticipated adverse reaction by customers to the planned price increases and store closures.

VALIDATING METRIC CHOICES

Think about how we determined the metrics—we used things like causal analysis. It is possible that the metrics we chose, in particular those for risk drivers and controls, were not the best ones; in fact, they may have been completely wrong. It is also possible that we set the strategic objective metric and the risk driver metric correctly but chose the wrong metric for the control. When you have sufficient historical data available, you should use that data to confirm your choice of metrics.

Earlier we discussed the notion of correlation, and I would just like to spend a little more time on that. When you have set the risk driver and control metrics properly, the movements in the values of those metrics should be highly correlated to the movement in the strategic objective metric. There are a couple of quick ways to gauge correlation; one way is to calculate it, the other way is to *view* it. Exhibit 8.7 shows the plots of the values for the three metrics over 10 periods.

From the exhibit, it is clear that there is a strong relationship between the value of the risk driver metric and the value of the strategic objective metric. It is equally clear that there is *not* a strong relationship between the value of the control metric and the value of the strategic objective metric. The correlation between the risk driver metric and the strategic objective metric is around 0.94, and the correlation between the control metric and

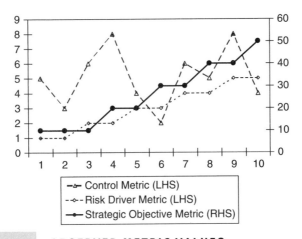

EXHIBIT 8.7   OBSERVED METRIC VALUES

the strategic objective metric is close to 0. Correlation can range from −1 to 1. Values around 0 represent low correlation, and values close to either −1 or 1 represent high correlation. Whether the correlation is positive or negative relates to the direction of movement; positive values mean the two variables generally move in the same direction, and negative values mean the two variables generally move in opposite directions. The lack of relationship between the values for the control metric and the strategic objective metric evident in this exhibit should lead you to question whether the metric you have chosen indeed represents a control in relation to the strategic objective metric.

REPORTING FINDINGS

Reports are an effective tool for stimulating reaction. In the SOAR process, this is indeed their primary purpose. A number of essential elements to reporting must exist to ensure maximum effectiveness of enterprise risk management:

- **Timeliness.** Results of the analysis must be disseminated within a time frame that makes them useful.
- **Accuracy.** No explanation should be needed here.
- **Appropriateness.** This element is about ensuring that the right person receives the information. By "right" I mean the recipient must, first, be able to understand the information and, second, be responsible for and/or capable of doing something about it. That is, this person must be the one responsible for and/or capable of performing the next step: reacting.

Because I find discussions about reporting boring, I will not cover the topic in detail here. It is pretty simple: You have to get the right information to the right person at the right time and present it in a way that is meaningful to him or her. Being responsible for enterprise risk management, you will know what constitutes the right information, whom the right people are, and appropriate time frames. What you will not be able to predefine is the last bit—the "right" way to present the information, so just go to the person and ask what he or she wants and be prepared to strongly argue against the old "traffic light" request; that's the one where a good result is represented by a green light, an average result is represented by an amber light and a poor result appears as a red light. The SOAR methodology prescribes the application of a reasonable degree of sophistication for risk quantification. To report that via a traffic light–type report will undervalue the process and reduce its effectiveness. In addition, allowing those people responsible for the react phase of the process to receive analytic results in such a simple format will hinder their ability to develop a deeper understanding of risk quantification, which surely is one of the goals of the enterprise risk management office.

The most effective way for the enterprise risk management office to report (current) risk is to show the (current) distributions of possible outcomes for each and every strategic objective. If you think that is overkill in your particular organization, by all means do something else. Very few organizations chase more than five strategic objectives at any time. You can report five distributions on a single Web page that should be immediately meaningful to the recipient. The Web page might look something like Exhibit 8.8.

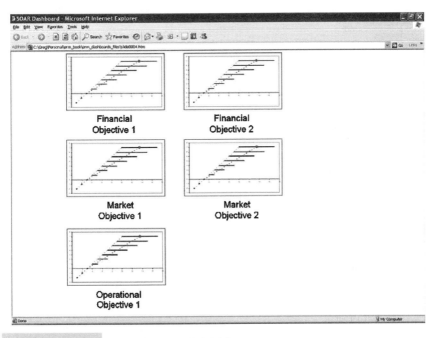

EXHIBIT 8.8   SOAR DASHBOARD

By inserting the word "current" in parentheses in the preceding paragraph, I have introduced the concept of time, which is not something we have discussed in great detail. I noted earlier that the SOAR process is iterative; that is, it is to be run continuously until your objective becomes an outcome. Over the time period associated with the objective, the risks and the associated events and possible outcomes may change. If you so desire, your reporting may include an analysis of the changing risk profile over time.

I will just take a moment to comment on a discussion on reporting in a 1999 publication from the RiskMetrics Group called "Risk Management—A Practical Guide." The authors state that "risk reports should be reasonably accurate." I believe that the report should be 100% accurate. I think what they are talking about is the data presented in the report, and they are recognizing that 100% accuracy is not required and may not even be possible. I support this view. The report, however, should be 100% accurate in its presentation of data, even though that data may not be 100% accurate. I guess I am being pedantic. I loathe reports and am frustrated every time someone asks "Can we get a report that shows this and that?" I consider reports as just the presentation of information. When people focus on what can be reported and how, sometimes they are missing the point. The point is not what can be reported and how, it is how the data that is being reported was generated. To produce a report in error—for example, because the data was not refreshed or because the report is picking up the wrong field from the database—is inexcusable. I minimize reports to presentation, while the authors from the RiskMetrics Group include the data and its preparation.

Having said that, I do not want to leave you with the impression that reports are completely useless. I do not mean that. Under the SOAR process, the primary purpose of the report is to stimulate a reaction. Another purpose is to reinforce the SOAR way of thinking (i.e., thinking in terms of a probability distribution of outcomes). I do not believe the traffic light system will achieve the first of these objectives, and it cannot achieve the second. Say someone demands that you supply a report including a traffic light. What would you expect the person's reaction to be to any of the report objects presented in Exhibit 8.9?

In Chapter 10 we discuss in detail a dial from the SOAR dashboard that I think conveys a great deal of valuable information. Include such a dial in the SOAR report. For now, I am just going to show a picture of it

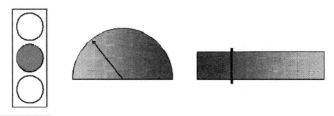

EXHIBIT 8.9   NOT-SO-VALUABLE REPORT OBJECTS

(Exhibit 8.10) and ask you to think about what you can gather from it. Imagine the metric is something easy like monthly profit (or loss), expressed in millions of dollars. Write down what you can glean from the graph.

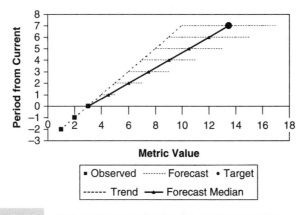

EXHIBIT 8.10   DIAL FROM THE SOAR DASHBOARD

Before we leave the analyze step, let us summarize what we have covered:

- The analyze step relates to the examination of metric values.
- Graphs will almost certainly play an important role in the analysis.
- Validation of data (i.e., observed values of metrics) is absolutely essential.
- The analysis must include an explanation of the movement in observed values of the metric(s) and justification of the forecast values.
- The analysis is to be reported to stimulate reaction.

CHAPTER 9

React to the Metric Analysis

O uch; this is where the "management" bit comes into play and things get a little more subjective. Remember that bit about "judicious management" at the beginning of this book? The SOAR process is designed to improve an organization's chance of attaining its strategic objectives. This is achieved by the application of discipline inherent within the SOAR process, in particular, the cyclical review of data and fact-based decision making. From the diagram of the SOAR process shown in Exhibit 6.2, you can see that the observe, analyze, and react steps within the process are circular. That is, you react based on the analysis, the analysis is based on the observations, and these steps are conducted a number of times over the life of the objective. Although it may surprise you, an alarmingly small proportion of organizations base their decisions, even those relating to strategic objectives, on valid data. An equally alarmingly high proportion of organizations fail to track their progress toward their strategic objectives. Application of the SOAR process overcomes these common failings and maximizes the organization's ability to achieve its strategic objectives. If you wish to rank the steps within the SOAR process from least important to most important, I would suggest that "react" is the most important because without reaction, the rest is a waste of time. In addition, the steps are complementary. Effective enterprise risk management can be achieved only by strict adherence to the entire process. I chose "react" as the most important step because this step can be considered as capturing the other steps as a set of assumptions within it; the thing you are reacting to is the analysis and you assume the analysis is valid, meaning it is based on the right data. I hope that you react following the application of "sound judgment." Whether you do or do not may be evident the next time you observe and analyze the relevant data!

As a reminder, the steps in the SOAR process that form the foundation of the SOAR methodology are:

1. Set (i.e., set metrics associated with strategic objectives)
2. Observe (i.e., observe metric values)
3. Analyze (i.e., analyze changes in metric values)
4. React (i.e., react to what the analysis reveals)

The SOAR process is a management process; the four steps constitute a process that helps you manage risks associated with striving to achieve strategic objectives. Do not confuse the management of the SOAR process with the role of managing the strategic plans themselves. Like any plans, strategic plans should have dedicated resources: project managers, sponsors, and so on. These people are led by the owner of the strategic objective. The SOAR methodology is designed for the enterprise risk management office, which is independent of any single project. The enterprise risk management office is the organization's guardian angel. When the organization treads on ice that is too thin, the enterprise risk management office must be there to call the organization back to safe ground.

We have reached the final step of the SOAR process without too much effort. Now let us have a quick recap on how we got here before we discuss what we do within this step. First we set metrics. This involves identifying metrics from each metric class and setting target values for the strategic objective metrics. We also have an option to set trigger values for the other metrics. Next we observe metric values. The only thing required in this second step is a little thought to determine the observation frequency, but even that is pretty straightforward. Within the third, analysis, step, we . . . analyze! The key is to pay attention to the detail. For example, do not assume that the data you have is correct; validate it. Check correlations between strategic objective metrics and control/risk driver metrics by plotting observed values and calculating correlations. Explain what has happened (i.e., explain the movements in the metrics) and justify your estimate of future values (which I suggested you refer to as the probability distribution of the metric value). Finally, in the fourth step, deliver a report (absent traffic lights) to the right person, so he or she can do what is described in this chapter.

The react step of the SOAR process applies to two groups of people: the enterprise risk management officers and the owners of the strategic objective. I have said it before: I advocate the execution of the SOAR process by a dedicated group of people assigned to the enterprise risk management office because I expect that those people who are assigned ownership of the strategic objectives will not (yet) be familiar with the SOAR methodology. The SOAR methodology sits over the top of the strategic objectives and monitors progress toward their achievement. The enterprise risk manager monitors progress in terms of the metrics defined under the SOAR process. The objective owner monitors progress according to whatever he or she likes *and* the reports supplied by the enterprise risk management office. Over time, the value of the SOAR methodology will be evident in the form of an increase in the number of objectives achieved, and the strategic objective owner will start to manage the objective under the SOAR methodology. At this time, the enterprise risk management office can be shut down.

Right, let us discuss the react step. Imagine we have assigned a single metric to a strategic objective, and values for that metric have been both forecast (for the duration of the period over which the objective is to be met) and observed (for the lapsed period since the objective was set). The plots of forecast and observed values for the metric appear in Exhibit 9.1, which repeats Exhibit 8.5.

What might be the reaction to this data? Well, the possibilities are endless, of course, and a number of them might involve cost cutting and retrenchment (even without knowing what the metric measures), but here are some reasonably foreseeable responses from senior management:

- "Great; we are ahead of forecast."
- "Great; we are ahead of forecast."
- "Great; we are ahead of forecast."

OK, enough of that. Some other responses might be:

- "Why is that solid line going all over the place?"
- "Could that solid line dip below the dashed line?"
- "We've exceeded forecast to date; let's hope that continues."

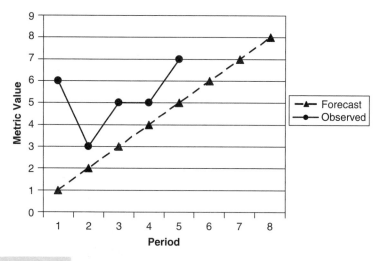

EXHIBIT 9.1   GRAPH OF FORECAST AND OBSERVED VALUES

In a second, we will discuss the type of questions the graph *should* invoke.

RECORD THE RATIONALE FOR YOUR REACTION

Record any actions, either planned or taken, and the rationale for those actions—and not just to protect your back! As a result of the analysis, you will decide to (not) take certain actions. In addition to detailing the (planned) actions, you should record both the rationale for your decisions and the expected outcomes, including time frames for completion. This record enables subsequent analysis of the quality of your decisions and serves to ensure that action does indeed get taken and that it has the desired effect.

SIMPLE TASK OF REACTING ACCORDING TO THE MEASURES

Exhibit 9.1 appeared earlier in Chapter 8 and at that time I suggested that senior management may view it positively. Let us consider what questions the exhibit should invoke.

There are several stunningly obvious and vital observations that should be made instantly, including:

- There is considerable volatility in observed values of this metric.
- There are several instances where the observed value of the metric differs very significantly from the predicted value.
- The metric does not exhibit any obvious pattern of behavior, and this is contrary to the prediction.

From these observations, these questions should arise:

- How do I know the data is accurate? (Of course, this question does not come from the exhibit; it is the question you should ask every single time someone presents you with data; think of it as healthy skepticism.)
- What are the possible future values of this metric, and what are the probabilities associated with each possible future value?
- What are the causes or drivers of the behavior of this metric?
- What impact does the movement in this metric have on our ability to achieve our strategic objective(s)?
- Why do the values for this metric differ so significantly from the predicted values?
- How are we ensuring that we use the information gained through the application of the measurement process to improve our chances of meeting our objective?

Equally important to knowing what questions to ask is having some reasonable idea of the nature of the answers that might result. Let us assume that this particular metric happens to be a key risk indicator; that is, it is a metric we have identified as being a leading indicator of risk, or a risk driver metric. When posing the questions above, consider these points:

- Data accuracy is often very hard to quantify. Ridiculous anomalies in the data should be readily identifiable; it is the slightly wrong stuff that is hard to see. You can make your life easier by assuming that slightly wrong data will not have a material impact on your outcome. The answer you are looking for might be something like "Extraordinary values are checked manually and removed if they are wrong," or maybe

"The data is reconciled to blah blah blah." What you do not want to hear is something like "We get it from the same system that we use to generate profit and loss so we assume it is correct." Yeah, right.

- Predictive models range from the very simple—things like trend lines—through to the reasonably complex—say, Monte Carlo simulation. Your enterprise risk management office should have access to human resources who know enough about statistics to identify and apply a reasonable approach to predicting future values, based on the data and modeling tools available. Let us assume you have no knowledge of statistics but wish to imagine what the solid line might look like over the remaining period. By simply looking at the solid line, we can note that, historically:
  - The solid line can go up or down or remain flat.
  - The biggest move has been −3 and the range of movement has been from −3 to 2.
  - The most common value is 5 (40% of observations are 5).
  - The most common move is 2 (50% of movements have been 2).

By applying a little basic math, we can build a simple predictive model based on this information. To do so, we simply translate that information into something we can apply in a model. We will represent the count of movements as a percentage of the total number of moves (which is 4):

Movement	Count (as %)
−3	25%
2	50%
0	25%

Now let us assume that those counts are likely to hold constant in the future; we could then express this "model" as shown next:

Movement	Probability
−3	25%
2	50%
0	25%

Period 5		Period 6		Period 7		Period 8
					2 (50%)	13
			2 (50%)	11	0 (25%)	11
					−3 (25%)	8
					2 (50%)	11
	2 (50%)	9	0 (25%)	9	0 (25%)	9
					−3 (25%)	6
					2 (50%)	8
			−3 (25%)	6	0 (25%)	6
					−3 (25%)	3
					2 (50%)	11
			2 (50%)	9	0 (25%)	9
					−3 (25%)	6
					2 (50%)	9
7	0 (25%)	7	0 (25%)	7	0 (25%)	7
					−3 (25%)	4
					2 (50%)	6
			−3 (25%)	4	0 (25%)	4
					−3 (25%)	1
					2 (50%)	8
			2 (50%)	6	0 (25%)	6
					−3 (25%)	3
					2 (50%)	6
	−3 (25%)	4	0 (25%)	4	0 (25%)	4
					−3 (25%)	1
					2 (50%)	3
			−3 (25%)	1	0 (25%)	1
					−3 (25%)	−2

EXHIBIT 9.2   PATHWAYS TO OUTCOMES

From this, we can build a tree of possible future values, which would look something like Exhibit 9.2.

The shaded cells show the possible values in future periods. Our model allows these moves: up by 2, flat and down by 3. We start from the most recently observed value, 7, and the model tells us that in the next period (period 6), the value of the metric could be 9 (= 7 + 2), 7 (= 7 + 0), or 4 (= 7 − 3). Moving forward, we can predict possible values (and their probability) out to period 8. Without the application of any sophisticated math (in fact, using nothing more than very basic math), we have predicted possible future values ranging from 13 to −2. Congratulations; you have just conducted a historical simulation analysis, albeit a very simple one. Having considered the possible paths the solid line may take, you are now in a better position to comprehend the analysis that your quantitative expert conducted. In the example, I have calculated the movement in the metric on an absolute basis (i.e., as the value in the current period minus the value in the previous period). I have done this for convenience only, and I do not mean to suggest that this is the most appropriate measurement of the movement. In fact, I believe it is *not* the most appropriate measure. Rather, we should use the percentage movement (i.e., calculate the movement by dividing the value in one period minus the value in the previous period by the value in the previous period). That is much easier to express mathematically:

$$\% \text{ move in metric } = (\text{metric value } (t) - \text{metric value } (t-1))/ \text{metric value } (t-1)$$

This discussion of historical simulation analysis could have been placed in Chapter 8 on the analyze step. I decided to place it here to convey a particular message: The enterprise risk manager and the owners of the strategic objectives must have a good enough understanding of the basic probability concepts discussed here to be able to fully understand what we have just done. Even though we are discussing basic probability concepts, I do not expect every strategic objective owner to have this understanding. It is the role of the enterprise risk management office to educate first the strategic objective owners and then every member of the organization. All members of the organization do not have to know all of its strategic objectives, of course, but progress toward achievement of "public" objectives should be publicized. Doing this has at least two effects: It helps everyone feel involved, and it increases the pressure on those striving to achieve the objective (which of course includes the officers of the enterprise risk management office).

Let us go back to the chart of forecast versus actual observations and view it slightly differently. Imagine that we are at the point in time when the forecast is made, before any metric values are observed. (By the way, you will not usually make a forecast without reference to any historical observations. In fact, it is more likely that values will be available; it is just that at the time the values were gathered, you did not recognize them as values of a metric; they were gathered in relation to something else.) At this point, the chart would lack the actual observations and would look like the one shown in Exhibit 9.3.

A more informative forecast, and one that far more clearly presents the possibility of variation in future values, could be depicted as shown in Exhibit 9.4.

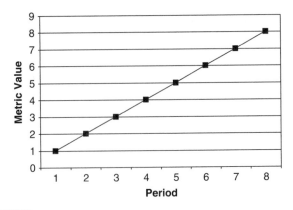

EXHIBIT 9.3   **GRAPH OF FORECAST VALUES**

This exhibit shows a distribution of possible outcomes (or forecast values) per period. Each bell-shape distribution has the metric value on the vertical axis and the probability (not shown) on the horizontal axis. (Note that in previous charts, the metric value was on the horizontal axis and the probability on the vertical axis. If the values are clearly labeled,

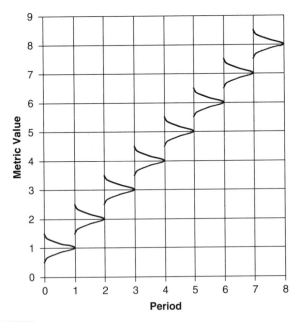

EXHIBIT 9.4   **GRAPH OF DISTRIBUTIONS OF FORECAST VALUES**

or described, it does not matter.) If you join the means of the distributions (which happen to coincide with the medians of the distribution), you get the straight line of the graph shown in Exhibit 9.3. Even though Exhibit 9.4 does not show the probabilities associated with the possible future values, it does provide some insight into the range of possible values for future periods. If we examine period 1, we can see that the predicted value for the metric at the end of the period is somewhere between 0.5 and 1.5 and the expected value (or mean of the distribution) is 1. Similarly, for period 2, the future value is predicted to be between 1.5 and 2.5 and the expected value is 2. If you were reading this online, you would be able to click on one of the lines and launch a pop-up window of that particular distribution, which would show the probabilities.

A reasonably common and well-founded belief is that uncertainty increases with time. For example, if you were asked how sure you are that you will still be alive tomorrow, you would probably be able to say that you are very sure (unless you are 107 years old and have a really bad cold). If you were asked how sure you are that you would still be alive in five years, your answer might be more along the lines of "Well, I'm healthy and am not into parachuting, so, barring any accidents, I reckon I've got a good chance" (unless you are 105 and regardless of your current state of health). This concept is also evident in the term structure of interest rates, which shows that people demand a higher rate of interest for locking their money away for a longer period of time. The demand for the higher interest rate is due at least in part to the concern that the organization will collapse before repaying the money and in part due to the fact that people are not sure whether they will need the money. There are few things in life that we can predict with the same confidence over different time intervals. In a more realistic forecast, the distributions would broaden in each future period, with the increasing breadth representing increasing uncertainty. That graph might look more like the one shown in Exhibit 9.5.

From this exhibit, we can see that the predicted values for the end of period 8 range from 6 to 10 and the expected value (or mean of the distribution, which happens to coincide with the median of the distribution) is (still) 8. This exhibit lends itself well to comparison against the values we calculated earlier via historical simulation. You will note that in that earlier model, we calculated possible future values ranging from −2 to 13. How is

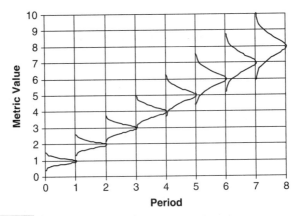

EXHIBIT 9.5   **ALTERNATE GRAPH OF DISTRIBUTIONS OF FORECAST VALUES**

this possible? Simple; we have applied two different models. The most significant difference between the two models is that the one presented in Exhibit 9.5 assumes a normal distribution of future values, while our earlier model was based on a skewed distribution.

There is an essential element of the SOAR process that I have not yet incorporated in the discussion about forecasts and that is that forecasts should be subject to regular review, as part of the SOAR process. In particular, the SOAR process demands regular observation and analysis of metric values and appropriate (re)action. At the end of the first period, the chart would look like the one in Exhibit 9.6, which shows the expected future value per period as opposed to the distribution of possible future values per period.

At the very least, following the SOAR process would lead you to review the forecast. Assume that achieving a metric value of 8 equates to achieving your strategic objective. (After all, that is what is required under the set step—you set a target value for the strategic objective metric that equates to achievement of the strategic objective.) When the observed value of the metric comes in at 6 at the end of the first period and you had forecast a value of 1, alarm bells should ring. Step 1 might be to compare the observed value (6) to the forecast *range* of possible values. If the range was, say, from 0.5 to 1.5 (as per Exhibit 9.5), then alarm bells should continue to

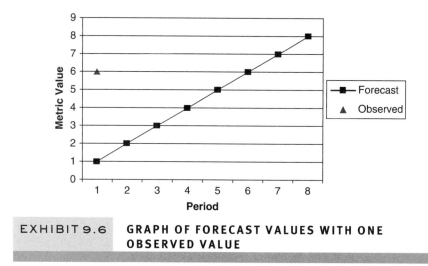

EXHIBIT 9.6   GRAPH OF FORECAST VALUES WITH ONE OBSERVED VALUE

ring. The gap between the forecast and actual values must be explained, or else you cannot rely on the forecast. When reviewing actual results, keep in mind that good is just as bad as bad and only average is good. Got it? I will explain.

The SOAR methodology recognizes and focuses on the fact that a range of outcomes is possible and prescribes a disciplined approach to monitoring indicators of those outcomes. Deviation from the forecast, whether above or below expectations, is evidence of variability; when I say "good is just as bad as bad," I mean that an observed value some distance above the expectation should be treated in the same way as an observed value equal distance below the expectation. When I say "only average is good," I mean that (only) observed values close to the expectation allow us some degree of relaxation; they suggest that we are on track (to achievement of the target value of the metric and, therefore, our strategic objective).

The SOAR methodology is designed to help the organization manage strategic objectives by managing the distribution of possible outcomes relating to those objectives. Quite simply, the methodology is designed to narrow and, if necessary, relocate the distribution of forecast values, as depicted in Exhibit 9.7.

Exhibit 9.8 compares some of the statistics associated with the two distributions depicted in Exhibit 9.7.

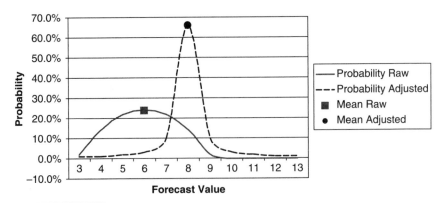

EXHIBIT 9.7   **INHERENT (RAW) AND RESIDUAL (CONTROLLED)
DISTRIBUTIONS**

CONFIDENCE

It is very common for a discussion on distributions to cover the subject of
confidence levels. Confidence levels are very useful when you are analyzing a distribution comprising a large number of data points. However, I do
not believe that the distributions you will encounter when applying the
SOAR process to strategic objectives will comprise a large number of
points. I base this reasoning on my belief that the distributions will almost
always be created via scenario analysis, which is a process that is not suitable
for creating a large set of data. In applying the SOAR method, the enterprise risk management officer needs to find the right balance between
theory and practice. This notion has been nicely expressed by Mintzberg
and Lampel:

**EXHIBIT 9.8   SUMMARY VALUES FROM INHERENT AND RESIDUAL
DISTRIBUTIONS**

Forecast Value	Probability Raw	Probability Adjusted
8	14%	66%
> 8	2%	17%
< 8	84%	17%
7 <= x <= 9	38%	86%

We need to ask better questions and generate fewer hypotheses—to allow ourselves to be pulled by real-life concerns rather than pushed by reified concepts. We need better practice, not neater theory.[1]

Let me provide a quick explanation of "confidence" as it relates to probability distributions. As you now know, the probability distribution is a plot of values and their associated probabilities. From the probability distribution, we can make observations like "There is a 1% probability that the value will be greater than 5." Another way to express this is "I am 99% sure that the result will be 5 or less." Yet another expression is "The maximum value, measured at the 99% confidence level, is 5." The confidence level is just a reference to the point in the distribution.

DIFFICULT TASK OF MANAGING HUMAN BEHAVIORS

Managing humans is not something I wish to discuss. I have lived and worked with humans for too long to believe that they can be understood. There is no way I am going to comment on how behaviors should be managed. I will do the least that I can and that is to let you know that appropriate management of people is absolutely essential to the achievement of strategic objectives. The enterprise risk management office can address this quite easily and without having any understanding of how to manage people. The enterprise risk management office should view people as just another source of risk to which metrics need to be attached. This is one area where the strategy map can really become a tangled web. The enterprise risk management office must apply the "keep it simple" principle. In particular, examine whether the people who have influence over the outcome of strategic objectives are truly motivated to achieve those outcomes; that is, are they free of any conflicting motivation? In conducting that analysis, be very, very careful. Consider, for example, the case where salespeople are financially motivated to sell units while the organization's objective is to increase sales revenue. According to the laws of supply and demand and price elasticity, you can imagine that some salespeople might offer units at a discounted price—a solution to their problem that may not be helpful for the people charged with increasing revenue. It is a simple, obvious conflict, but the startling fact is that it is remarkably common.

As an enterprise risk management executive, your immediate question should be: How does that happen? I will answer that very good question for you. Quite simply, organizations worldwide are generally run very poorly; only a very small number of organizations are well managed with respect to the achievement of their strategic objectives. Just think of any organization with which you have conducted business: your bank, the political party governing your state and country, your local government, your child's school, your medical insurer, the local take-away store, the organization that just advertised a product on television. Ask yourself these questions:

- From your interaction with that organization, can you imagine what its strategic objectives might be?
- Do you think the interaction you have had with that organization has been recorded as data that it will use for the management of its strategic objectives?
- Do you believe that the organization knows how to analyze the data available to it in order to manage its strategic objectives?
- Do you think the organization has the skill to manage its strategic objectives?

At this point I will make my second and final detour into human behavior to highlight how carefully questions need to be posed and answers need to be interpreted. I strongly urge you to give this subject further thought—but not too much lest you get lost in this fascinating field. The subject to which I refer is the measurement of an individual's risk appetite/aversion. The issue is brilliantly covered in a paper entitled "Prospect Theory: An Analysis of Decision under Risk" by Daniel Kahneman and Amos Tversky.[2] They demonstrate how people's choices are impacted by their perception of risk/reward and that their perception of risk/reward is at least partly formed by how the context is defined. Kahneman and Tversky employ an example similar to this one:

This question is posed to a group of people:

A disease that could kill 600 people may be handled by either option A or B. Option A will guarantee that 200 lives are saved. Under option B, there is a 33% chance that no one will die and a 67% chance that everyone will die. Would you choose option A or B?

This question is posed to a second group of people:

A disease that could kill 600 people may be handled by either option C or D. Under option C, 400 people will die. Under option D, there is a 33% chance that no one will die and a 67% chance that everyone will die. Would you choose option C or D?

Let us make seven observations:

1. Option A saves 200 lives (kills 400).
2. Option C kills 400 people (saves 200).
3. Options A and C are the same.
4. Under option B, there is a 33% chance that everyone will live and a 67% chance that everyone will die.
5. Under option D, there is a 33% chance that everyone will live and a 67% chance that everyone will die.
6. Options B and D are the same.
7. From a statistical point of view, each option boasts the same expected loss of life: 400 people.

Let us ignore the last point for one second and imagine what sort of results we might expect from the two different groups, based not on a reading of the question but based on the first six points. First, I would expect that roughly the same proportion of people from the first group choose option A as the proportion of people from the second group who choose C. Would you? Second, I can imagine that people may view options A and B (or C and D) differently, and I could imagine an unbalanced response. Surprisingly, here are the results:

- From group 1, 72% chose option A and 28% chose option B.
- From group 2, 22% chose option C and 78% chose option D.

Kahneman and Tversky draw these conclusions:

- People place greater emphasis on losses than on gains.
- People prefer certainty to possibilities.

What are the implications for the SOAR methodology? One implication is that people are likely to pay less attention to observed metric values that are higher than the forecast value, which could be dangerous, as understanding higher-than-expected values is just as important as understanding lower-than-expected values. The enterprise risk management office must ensure that reactions to observations of metric values are appropriate. The variation in responses suggests that people generally struggle with the concept of probability. This point is very important in terms of acceptance of the SOAR methodology. The enterprise risk management office always must communicate enterprise risk management concepts in terms of the (probability) distribution of possible outcomes. That one conclusion of the research was that people prefer certainty tells us how we should promote the SOAR methodology: as a method that aims to reduce uncertainty (which is lucky, because that is exactly what it is!). The enterprise risk management office always must communicate in terms of the probability distribution of possible outcomes, and it constantly must remind people that the office is trying to achieve a reduction in the uncertainty of outcomes. We know that a reduction in uncertainty translates to a thinning of the distribution around the target value of the strategic objective metric.

You have made it! We are at the end of the process. By now I am quite sure you remember the steps, but I am going to throw in another copy of the SOAR process flow diagram and summarize each step.

The SOAR process is represented in the process flow diagram shown in Exhibit 9.9.

The four steps of the SOAR process are:

1. *Set.* Define metrics for each of the stated strategic objectives. I recommend that you define at least one metric for each of the three metric classes. The SOAR methodology demands that you set a target value for the strategic objective metric. Also consider trigger values for risk driver and control metrics.

2. *Observe.* Observe and record metric values at whatever frequency you have deemed appropriate.

3. *Analyze.* Analyze movements in metric values in order to understand them and forecast future values. Also, report our findings.

4. *React.* The officers of the enterprise risk management office and the owners of the strategic objectives do something in response to what the analysis reveals.

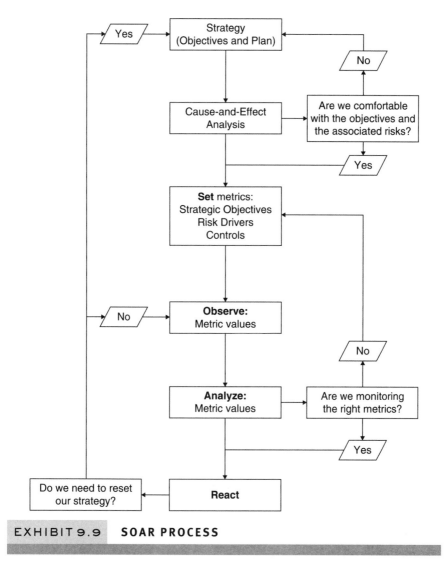

EXHIBIT 9.9   SOAR PROCESS

NOTES

1. H. Mintzberg and J. Lampel, "Reflecting on the Strategy Process," in M. Cusumano and C. Markides, eds., *Strategic Thinking for the Next Economy* (Jossey-Bass, 2001).
2. D. Kahneman and A. Tversky, "Prospect Theory: An Analysis of Decision Under Risk," *Econometrica* 47 (March 1979): 263–291.

CHAPTER 10

SOAR Dashboard

Despite my dislike of the word "dashboard," primarily due to the vast array of totally inadequate examples I have seen, I believe that, when correctly designed, a dashboard can be a very useful tool. There is an incredibly popular misconception that enterprise risk management can be achieved by providing senior management a dashboard of risks measured by business units. Some view a dashboard containing n dials as being equivalent to enterprise risk management. n might represent the number of business units or divisions within the organization, or the different types of risks they believe they face (and manage). This approach is far from effective and evidences a naive view of enterprise risk management. More generally, a dashboard approach, where the dials represent ordinary operational activities (such as the measurement of credit exposure or the number of pins produced to acceptable standard), is not appropriate for enterprise risk management.

TODAY'S DASHBOARD

I spent just a moment considering whether "Today's Dashboard" was the right title for this section, and I would just like to spend about the same amount of time explaining my rationale for choosing it. By "today," I mean "current," but I did not want to use an expression that might imply something very dynamic. I believe that the word "dashboard" carries a connotation of a live instrument that twitches in near real time, like the speedometer of a moving car. Although this is usually how a dashboard dial behaves, I do not believe it is appropriate in the context of enterprise risk

| Market Risk | Credit Risk | Operational Risk |

EXHIBIT 10.1   EXAMPLE OF A POOR-QUALITY ENTERPRISE RISK MANAGEMENT DASHBOARD

management, as the dashboard typically is giving us a view on slow-moving metrics that must be measured over a medium to long term, relating to medium- to long-term outcomes.

Enterprise risk management should employ a dashboard where each dial represents a strategic objective, not some operational aspect of running the organization. If you are a bank, for example, Exhibit 10.1 would be completely inappropriate as an enterprise risk management dashboard.

For *any* organization, Exhibit 10.2 (assuming it includes the supporting details) would be a useful resource for the enterprise risk management officer.

Let us investigate one of the panels in a little more detail to understand what information it reveals. Exhibit 10.3 is the same as one of those presented in Exhibit 10.2, except that the legend is displayed. (It is also the same as Exhibit 8.10. At that time I asked you to write down any observations you could make from the graph. Did you do it? I hope so. Now is your last chance to check whether you have gained a reasonable understanding of what has been discussed throughout the book. Before continuing, write down some observations if you have not yet done so.)

What information can you draw from Exhibit 10.3, and what questions should that information invoke?

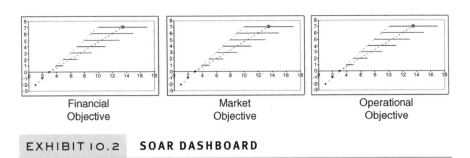

| Financial Objective | Market Objective | Operational Objective |

EXHIBIT 10.2   SOAR DASHBOARD

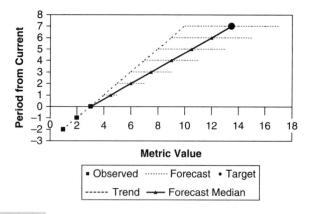

EXHIBIT 10.3   DIAL FROM THE SOAR DASHBOARD

Let us start with some observations that can be drawn directly from the plot of the data:

- We have been running the SOAR process for three periods, and the observed values of the metric have been 1, 2, and 3.
- There are seven periods remaining in the term of the strategic objective.
- If the observed trend continues, the metric will reach 10 in seven periods from now.
- The target value for the metric is 13.5 (a bit hard to tell, I know, but if this was online, you would be able to hover over the large dot and the pop-up would give you this figure.)
- The observed trend aligns with the minimum forecast values.

What inferences can be drawn?

- Probably the most significant one is that our forecast appears optimistic; that is, the forecast values are higher than what we might expect based on the trend drawn from historical observations.
- If the trend drawn from historical observations continues, we will not reach our target (i.e., we will not achieve our objective).

What information is not available that might be helpful?

- Forecast values for the first three (now-elapsed) periods, so that we could see whether those were accurate.

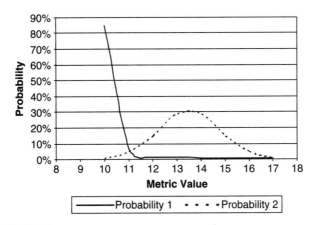

EXHIBIT 10.4   UNDERLYING PROBABILITY DISTRIBUTIONS

- Probabilities associated with the forecast values. Imagine that the distributions shown in Exhibit 10.4 represent two different distributions of the values forecast in the ultimate period. Which one would give you more confidence that you will achieve your target (metric) value of 13.5?

  (By the way, by now you should be able to recognize that the line representing probability 1 in the exhibit does not coincide with the forecast median in the Exhibit 10.3. Turn back and have a look. In the Exhibit 10.3, the median is 13.5. In Exhibit 10.4, the median of probability 1 is the value at the extreme left of the line, somewhere around 10. If our forecast was as per probability 1, there would be greater alignment between that forecast and the trend line, but we would be very worried about failing to meet the target value. The line referred to as probability 2 aligns with the forecast in Exhibit 10.3 and represents a greater chance of success, but leaves us wondering about the difference between this forecast and the trend line.)

- Reasons why the forecast values are greater than the trend drawn from observed values.

What questions might you pose and what types of answers should you expect?

- Question: Is the data accurate? Answer: Yes, let me explain the process that I followed to validate the data. Blah, blah, blah.

- Question: Do we expect the trend drawn from observed values to continue? Answer: No, we expect future values to fall close to our median forecast values. The reasons for this are blah, blah, blah.

- Question: Can you show me the probability distribution of forecast values for the remaining periods? Answer: Yes, of course. (The analyst should then click on the screen to invoke the distribution for a particular period.)

- Question: Have we assessed whether we need to revise the forecast? Answer: Yes, here is a copy of my analysis.

- Question: What action do you recommend we take in order to give our organization the best chance of meeting our objective? Answer: By applying the SOAR methodology, we have created a set of circumstances that results in a high probability of meeting our objective. I highly recommend we continue to follow the SOAR process. (Response from manager who posed the question: "Pure genius! I will give you a 50% pay raise effective immediately.")

SOAR Black Box Recorder

The black box flight recorder, conceived by Dr. David Warren, was introduced to the world through the field of aviation in the late 1950s. An equivalent tool is required for effective enterprise risk management. The objective of the tool, when applied to enterprise risk management, is the same as when applied in aviation: to record decisions and the context in which they were made. In the field of enterprise risk management, the black box takes the form of a database, and it records the data surrounding the decisions made by the enterprise risk management officers.

CHAPTER 11

Existing Enterprise Risk Management Approaches

In this chapter I discuss a few popular models that are *used* for enterprise risk management, even though not all of them have been designed for that purpose; rather, they were designed for some other purpose and people have chosen to apply them to enterprise risk management. As a direct result of not having been designed for it, they are not particularly useful when applied to enterprise risk management.

More generally, I take this opportunity to distinguish between risk management and compliance. Quite simply, risk management is a science and compliance is an exercise. They are worlds apart, and they should stay that way. Failure to comply with something is a risk that you may wish to monitor, perhaps by adherence to the SOAR methodology.

SIX SIGMA

A surprising number of individuals who should know better see the Six Sigma methodology as being equivalent to enterprise risk management. That is, if you ask this group of people to name some enterprise risk management methodologies, Six Sigma will be among them. Six Sigma is not an enterprise risk management methodology. It is a quality assurance framework and has no *direct* application to enterprise risk management. Six Sigma has application to achieving improvements in operations, which should increase your chances of achieving certain *operational* objectives.

BALANCED SCORECARD

The balanced scorecard is currently the most popular proxy for enterprise risk management. It is probably the one that could most closely be defined as the standard. So it is worth some attention, as the SOAR methodology aims to take the place of the balanced scorecard. Organizations using a balanced scorecard often recognize that it is not an enterprise risk management vehicle; they have chosen to apply it in the absence of something better. The balanced scorecard has its origins in a study on performance management.[1] Some elements of the balanced scorecard have direct application to enterprise risk management, such as the strategy map and the employment of cause-and-effect analysis. Most likely by design (i.e., by virtue of its focus on performance measurement), the balanced scorecard as popularized by Robert Kaplan and David Norton does not adequately prescribe how to manage risk. Performance is an outcome, and enterprise risk management is about taking action that is intended to (favorably) influence outcomes, so enterprise risk management precedes performance, performance measurement, and the balanced scorecard. When you are operating an effective enterprise risk management framework, this will be evident in the performance measures reported via your balanced scorecard. So when I say that the SOAR methodology replaces the balanced scorecard, I mean it replaces the balanced scorecard implemented for enterprise risk management. I fully expect the balanced scorecard to maintain its earned position as the standard for performance management, and I find it hard to imagine anyone trying to implement the SOAR methodology for performance management. The balanced scorecard is a good tool for answering the question: How well have we done? The SOAR methodology is designed to answer the question: How are we going to do?

COSO

As with the other approaches, it is important to keep in mind the intention of the Committee of Sponsoring Organizations (COSO) when examining the application of the COSO framework to enterprise risk management. The Committee of Sponsoring Organizations of the Treadway Commission is "dedicated to improving the quality of financial reporting."[2] So should we expect it to be completely effective as an enterprise risk management framework?

The definition of enterprise risk management contained within the COSO document very closely aligns with my own definition. COSO defines enterprise risk management as:

> A process, effected by an entity's board of directors, management and other personnel, applied in strategy setting and across the enterprise, designed to identify potential events that may affect the entity, and manage risk to be within its risk appetite, to provide reasonable assurance regarding the achievement of entity objectives.

The similarities are:

- We both define enterprise risk management as a process.
- We both see application to setting strategy (of course, this is also a difference, as the SOAR methodology is more focused on the application of enterprise risk management to the *execution* of strategy as opposed to the setting of strategy).
- We both see it as applying across the enterprise.
- We both see it being employed to identify adverse events.
- We both see it being employed to help the organization achieve its objectives.

My personal disappointment with the COSO framework is that beyond the definition of enterprise risk management, it offers little guidance on how to design and execute an effective enterprise risk management framework. As I advocate, COSO views variation in outcomes as a proxy for risk. COSO does not offer any definition of the term "risk"; it does, however, define "risk tolerances":

> Risk tolerances are the acceptable levels of variation relative to the achievement of objectives.

This definition aligns to my own comments on desirability of outcomes. Beyond having similar definitions of risk and enterprise risk management, the COSO framework and the SOAR methodology have little in common. This is because the COSO framework does not define a methodology for measuring risk.

■ NOTES

1. Nolan Norton Institute, "Measuring Performance in the Organization of the Future," 1990.
2. http://www.coso.org/

CHAPTER 12

Regulation and Compliance

G iven the volume of prevailing regulations designed to treat risk, it is appropriate to examine their application to enterprise risk management. In this chapter we look at a number of contemporary regulatory frameworks and popular organizational approaches and consider their application to enterprise risk management. We will find that none of the frameworks comes close to having strong application to enterprise risk management, primarily by design: None of the frameworks has been designed to manage the risks associated with strategic objectives.

SARBANES-OXLEY ACT

Let me be very clear on this: Internal audit and enterprise risk management have very little in common. The Sarbanes-Oxley Act[1] sits firmly within the internal audit field and offers very little to enterprise risk management. Expressed most simply, Sarbanes-Oxley is a set of rules relating to due diligence in the preparation of financial statements. Wow; what an amazing idea! Here is my version of Sarbanes-Oxley: Directors should check stuff before they sign stuff off.

You may recall that within the SOAR methodology, we define a group of "corporate governance" objectives within the "operational" category of objectives. If you like, you can stick Sarbanes-Oxley in that group. These excerpts from Section 404 are the most interesting requirements under Sarbanes-Oxley:

> [E]stablishing and maintaining an adequate internal control structure and procedures for financial reporting.

[A]ssessment, as of the end of the most recent fiscal year of the issuer, of the effectiveness of the internal control structure and procedures of the issuer for financial reporting.

Let us convert those requirements to a strategic objective and then consider the metrics we might define and employ under the SOAR process. The objective could be stated as:

To produce financial reports that are at least 99% accurate.

What should be the strategic objective metric? The percentage of accurate data in the financial reports.

What could be a risk driver metric? The percentage of accurate data in the first draft of the financial reports.

What could be a control metric? The percentage of data that has been subject to independent validation.

Basel II

Basel II[2] is a set of guidelines designed to ensure that banks hold an acceptable minimum level of capital to protect those banks (well, more correctly, their depositors) against losses resulting from adverse consequences of market, credit, and operational risk. Senior management in some banks believe that monitoring market, credit, and operational risk management processes is equivalent to enterprise risk management. I do not expect to see these banks achieving their strategic objectives.

AS/NZS 4360:2004: Risk Management

AS/NZS 4360 provides a reasonable overview to enterprise risk management and is a useful guideline. However, as you might expect from a guideline, it does not prescribe a complete methodology. Like COSO, it provides some useful definitions and a strong skeleton, but it lacks flesh and blood.

Organizational Risk Management Policy

It is impossible for me to comment on the quality of your current organizational risk management policy. If it is based on one of the other frameworks I have mentioned here, I can imagine your policy will boast some of the characteristics of that framework. Regardless the quality of your policy, congratulations for having one.

■ NOTES

1. Sarbanes–Oxley Act, 2002, United States.
2. Basel Committee on Banking Supervision, Bank for International Settlements, "International Convergence of Capital Measurement and Capital Standards" (June 2006).

CHAPTER 13

Application of the Concept of "Shifting the Distribution"

The SOAR methodology aims to drive a shift in the distribution of possible outcomes to produce a set of (controlled) possible outcomes that is more favorable to the organization. We have talked about creating a thinner, taller distribution located around the organization's desired outcome. In this chapter, I offer some examples of the application of this concept, though not under the SOAR methodology.

GE

The concept of shifting the distribution has been applied very successfully by one of the world's largest organizations, General Electric Company (GE), albeit not directly to the achievement of strategic objectives.

In his autobiography, Jack Welch, former Chairman and CEO of GE, describes—and even draws—the "vitality curve."[1] By both definition and appearance, it is a reasonably normal distribution similar to those described earlier in this book and applied within the SOAR methodology. As opposed to being a distribution of possible outcomes, it is a distribution of people, where the distribution is divided into three sections referred to as the "top 20," the "vital 70," and the "bottom 10." Welch states that individuals in the "bottom 10" (i.e., the underperformers) "generally had to go." This cull is similar to the SOAR concept of shifting the distribution, and the intent is the same: to create a more favorable distribution.

In a way that resembles the use of metrics within the SOAR process, the process around the Welch vitality curve includes the use of metrics, collectively referred to as "the four Es of GE leadership." Evidently, an individual who boasts high levels of *energy*, a great ability to *energize* others, the *edge*, and an ability to *execute* will be more likely to appear in the top 20 than the bottom 10.

Bank Treasury Operations

Dealing rooms of banks worldwide not only apply but *rely* on the concept of shifting the distribution to run their businesses. The science of hedging is a prime example. When a dealer takes a position on some market-related instrument, say an interest rate swap, he or she exposes the organization to the risks associated with that exposure, including the risk of financial loss due to an adverse movement in interest rates. That is the inherent risk. Often the bank will reduce this risk/exposure (whatever you want to call it) by taking an offsetting position. This has the result of shifting the distribution and leaves the organization exposed to the residual risk.

Humans in Daily Life

I have included daily life examples throughout this book to help readers recognize that the SOAR methodology is not some impractical theoretical rhetoric. In fact, the SOAR methodology is just an articulation of a disciplined approach to applying what most of us do on a daily basis. When driving a car, for example, you make decisions based on the distribution of possible outcomes (albeit that your decision may not be made after robust analysis of those outcomes). When driving along a suburban street, for example, you probably are likely to drive at a modest speed. You are unlikely to drive at, say, twice the legal limit but might exceed the limit by a bit (intentionally or otherwise). Most likely your decision not to drive at a speed double the legal limit has something to do with the amount and probability of a penalty, the probability and severity of an accident, and possibly the fact that your car cannot go that fast. The distributions of possible outcomes might look something like Exhibit 13.1.

If indeed the distributions of possible outcomes did look like those in Exhibit 13.1, most rational humans usually would adhere to the limit and

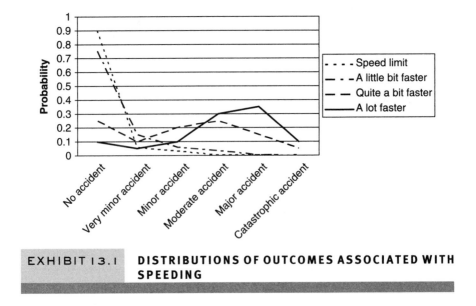

EXHIBIT 13.1   **DISTRIBUTIONS OF OUTCOMES ASSOCIATED WITH SPEEDING**

possibly breach it by traveling "a little bit faster" if they had some need to do so. It would be difficult to imagine a set of circumstances that could justify traveling "quite a bit faster" or "a lot faster" than the limit. By making a decision to slow down if you notice that you are driving above the limit, you are shifting the distribution.

AIRLINES

Immediately after 9/11, airlines and airports around the world reviewed and, in most cases, changed their procedures in order to reduce the possibility of a similar event. Note that in the discussion about driving a car, I mentioned both the likelihood and severity of an outcome; here I mention only the likelihood (or probability). In fact, most airlines did make changes to address severity as well, but the fact is that if someone succeeds in a plan to execute an act of terrorism that involves a plane, not much can be done to reduce the severity. So, quite rightly, resources were devoted to reducing the probability of undesired outcomes. Measures such as no hand luggage and more thorough screening of passengers and checked-in luggage were introduced. Importantly, the measures were applied on a prioritized basis; that is, flights more likely to be targeted were treated more

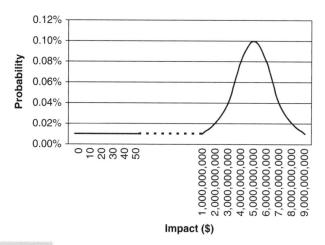

EXHIBIT 13.2   **LOSS DISTRIBUTION DUE TO TERRORIST ACT**

carefully. Consider, for example, an Australian airline. Would you expect that airline to introduce the same safety measures on flights between Perth and Broome as it does for flights between Sydney and New York? I would not, on the basis that terrorists are less likely to target the Perth-to-Broome flight, as that act would not generate sufficient publicity (and fear).

Let us consider what the distribution of possible outcomes for flights between London and New York might have looked like immediately after 9/11 (i.e., including what we learned from that day). It might have looked something like Exhibit 13.2. (in which I have assigned a dollar value to human life, so the "impact" is the dollar value of lives lost and physical assets destroyed).

As a result of the introduction of the safety measures, the residual distribution might look something like Exhibit 13.3.

One Other Example

Finally:

> In 1984, William Ruckelshaus, head of the US Environmental Protection Agency, mandated that the uncertainty surrounding each risk estimate be "expressed as distributions of estimates and not as magic numbers

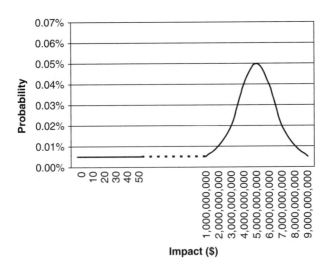

EXHIBIT 13.3   ADJUSTED (CONTROLLED OR RESIDUAL) LOSS DISTRIBUTION DUE TO TERRORIST ACT

that can be manipulated without regard to what they really mean . . . One way to improve our success in managing software-related risk is to use distributions, and to base them on historical data, not just on expert judgement."[2]

■ NOTES

1. J. Welch and J. Byrne, *Jack—Straight from the Gut* (Headline Book Publishing, 2001).
2. W. Ruckelshaus, "Risk in a Free Society," *Risk Analysis* 4 (1984): 161, cited in S. Pfleeger, "Risky Business: What We Have Yet To learn about Risk Management," *Journal of Systems and Software* 53 (2000): 265–273.

CHAPTER 14

Implementing the SOAR Methodology

I f you have reached this point and understood all that you have read, then you have nothing to fear; implementing the SOAR methodology is easy. We will now consider what is required to implement the SOAR methodology, including a very brief overview of applying the SOAR process, with a more detailed discussion of applying the SOAR process a little later.

The SOAR methodology comprises these components:

- Strategic objectives
- Enterprise risk management office
- SOAR process

As we have done so far, we will assume that strategic objectives have been conceived and stated, so we will discuss the other elements.

RESOURCING THE ENTERPRISE RISK MANAGEMENT OFFICE

I have no intention of talking about things like printers and pens. The only resources that are unique to the enterprise risk management office established under the SOAR methodology are the human resources. Like every functional unit within an organization, the enterprise risk management office should define and adhere to policies and procedures and employ standard documentation to the greatest extent possible. Here we discuss just two types of resource: people and technology.

Enterprise Risk Management Officers

I have previously stated that the human resources of the enterprise risk management office are vital to the success of your enterprise risk management program. Accordingly, the SOAR methodology includes an education program and certification process for enterprise risk management officers, designed to ensure that those officers have a common understanding of and consistently apply the SOAR methodology. In this section I will discuss the attributes an enterprise risk management officer must possess in order to apply the SOAR process effectively. The enterprise risk management officer must:

- Be conversant in simple probability distributions, such as those described in this book.
- Be able to conduct and present an analysis of metric values.
- Be able to lead workshops in which possible future outcomes are considered.
- Be able to conduct analyses to determine causes and consequences.
- Be able to conceive control mechanisms.
- Have the personal skills to be able to hold meaningful conversations with stakeholders.

Enabling Technology

Success of the SOAR methodology does not rely on complex, expensive technology. Rather, the SOAR methodology can be implemented effectively on simple, cheap technology that you likely already possess and perhaps even use within your organization. Whatever technology you use to support your enterprise risk management program, I recommend you choose technology that boasts these characteristics:

- Easy to use
- Popular (i.e., it is already widely used, and not necessarily for enterprise risk management)

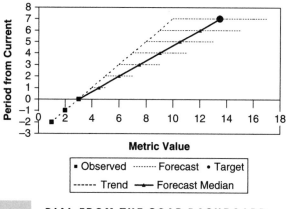

EXHIBIT 14.1   **DIAL FROM THE SOAR DASHBOARD**

- Can accept and store data
- Can present data
- Reliable

When deciding on the enabling technology, keep in mind that it will not have to do anything remarkable and that its primary function is to record your application of the SOAR process. You will need to record numbers (in particular metric values) and text (such as statements of strategic objectives and the content of the analyses conducted). In addition, you will need to generate and present numbers, graphs, and text.

My use of the phrase "easy to use" may appear flippant and far from reality. I do not wish to define the expression, as I believe that it is highly subjective. However, I will offer a couple of examples of how information might be presented and used within the application of the SOAR process. Recall the dial from the SOAR dashboard shown in Chapter 10? It is repeated here as Exhibit 14.1.

One of the questions this might invoke, as discussed earlier, is: Can I see the probability distribution for the forecast for period n? Ideally, your enabling technology would present this to you at the click of a mouse; you would hover over the range of forecast values and invoke a pop-up menu with a right mouse-click and one of the menu items would be "view probability distribution." On selection of that option, Exhibit 14.2 would appear.

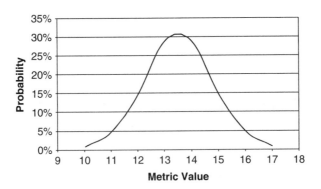

EXHIBIT 14.2   **PROBABILITY DISTRIBUTION BEHIND A DIAL OF THE SOAR DASHBOARD**

There are approximately a gazillion appropriate technologies and at least as many inappropriate ones. I cannot imagine your information technology staff having too much trouble recommending suitable technologies.

APPLYING THE SOAR PROCESS

The SOAR process has been the focus of this book. In this section I will just present a quick overview of what you already know.

Let us just reflect on the SOAR process:

1. Set metrics associated with objectives.

2. Observe metric values.

3. Analyze changes in metric values.

4. React to what the analysis reveals.

To set metrics, you must conduct both causal (or why, why, why?) and cause-and-effect analyses. I highly recommend that you also classify the metrics you have agreed on into these classes: key risk indicator metrics, control indicator metrics, and strategic objective metrics. Recall that the discussion around classification is at least as important as the classification itself. The greatest purpose served by any classification system in existence is nothing more than convenience. So do not worry if your discussion leads to agreement to disagree and you end up arbitrarily assigning the metric to one of the classes. You usually only have to decide between two, as the metrics for strategic objectives will rarely be mistaken for metrics for

EXHIBIT 14.3   SAMPLE METRICS

Strategic Objective	Strategic Objective Metric	Key Risk Indicator Metric	Control Indicator Metric
Reduce the instance of malaria in Africa	Cases of malaria (count)	Number of mosquito larvae (count)	Area sprayed for mosquito larvae (sq km)
Outstanding customer service	Customer satisfaction metric (number)	Customer complaints (percent)	Staff trained in customer service (percent)
Increase market share	Market share (%)	Sales ($)	Advertising expense ($)
			Sales training (count of attendees)
Increase profit	Net profit ($)	Revenue ($) Expenses ($)	Expenses ($)

controls or risks. It is most likely that group members will be divided by metrics that some think could be classified as control indicator metrics while others think they are risk indicator metrics. Now, some of you may be wondering how these two classes can ever cause confusion, because they seem so distinct to you. In most cases, that is true. Exhibit 14.3 presents some examples.

In the exhibit, there does not seem to be any confusion. But imagine if I had decided to classify the count of the number of mosquito larvae as a control indicator metric in relation to the strategic objective of reducing the instance of malaria. Does it matter? No. We will observe the same relationship between the control indicator metric and the strategic objective metric as we would observe between the key risk indicator metric and the strategic objective metric, because it is the same thing, just with a different label. So I will say it again: Do not get too excited about the *classification* of metrics. Remember that setting a strategic objective metric includes determining the metric and its target value. Setting control/risk indicator metrics involves determining the metric and might require setting trigger values. As a rule of thumb, if you get stuck when trying to classify a metric as either a control or a risk driver, consider the origin of the object. Is it something that someone has put in place, or is it something that just happens to be there? Almost certainly, if it is something that someone has put in place, it is a control. Quite likely, something that just happens to be there is a risk driver.

After the set step, you must observe metric values. To observe current values, you need to capture data.

After the observe step, you must analyze metric values.

Finally, you must react.

That's how you *apply* the SOAR process.

CHAPTER 15

SOAR in Action Example

I n this chapter we are going to walk through an example of SOAR in action. The strategic objective to which we will apply the SOAR methodology is:

> To increase annual sales over the next six years to achieve sales of $100 million in 2013.

The purpose of this example is to give you a taste of what it will be like to operate under the SOAR methodology. From this example, you should see that operation under the SOAR methodology will not be a significant burden and, most important, it will improve the likelihood of achieving your objective.

For the purpose of this example, we will use these players:

- Mr. Distribution, the enterprise risk manager
- Ms. Objective, the person responsible for the strategic objective and the strategic plan

Step 1. Set (Metrics)

We begin by confirming the *meaning* of the statement of objective:

> To increase annual sales over the next six years to achieve sales of $100 million in 2013.

There are two important elements to the objective:

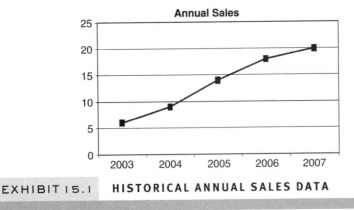

EXHIBIT 15.1   HISTORICAL ANNUAL SALES DATA

1. To achieve annual sales of $100 million in 2013

2. To increase annual sales over the next six years

The first thing we need to do is confirm our starting point. To do so, let us examine the history of annual sales. Assume annual sales in preceding years are as shown in Exhibit 15.1.

It seems reasonable to take $20 million as our starting point. We can immediately add to the graph, the strategic objective target value. Note that we have not yet defined the strategic objective metric, although it looks like the metric will be annual sales. The graph can be modified to include the strategic objective target value and will appear as shown in Exhibit 15.2.

It is not clear from the statement of strategic objective whether the values of annual sales for the interim years (i.e., 2008 to 2012) are important, although we can gather that a gradual increase is sought. In the real world, we would look to see if the business plan gave us any clues, and we would look to align to that. In this case, where there is no business plan, we will make something up. The desired path(s) to the target level of $100 million might be represented as shown in Exhibit 15.3.

In this exhibit, the values for path 1 have been determined by simple linear estimation (between the start and end points). The values in path 2 have been determined by imagining that the trend might be hard to shake in the short term, so values for the first two periods of the objective period have been estimated to align with the existing trend. As you can see, path 2

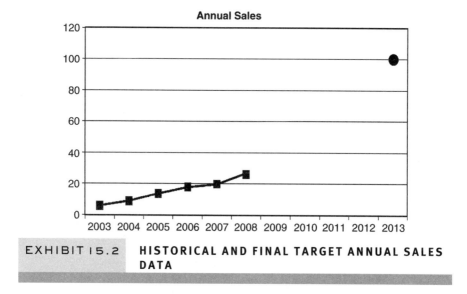

EXHIBIT 15.2   **HISTORICAL AND FINAL TARGET ANNUAL SALES DATA**

requires acceleration in sales growth over the objective period. By the way, to get an idea of the hard work that lies ahead, I recommend adding a trend line to the historical observations and comparing (visually) the trend to the possible paths. Exhibit 15.4 shows what it looks like in our case.

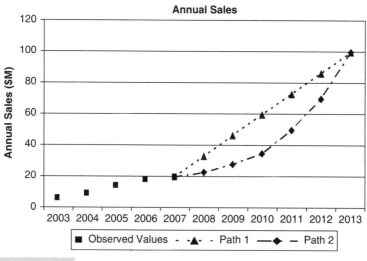

EXHIBIT 15.3   **TWO POSSIBLE PATHS TO THE TARGET**

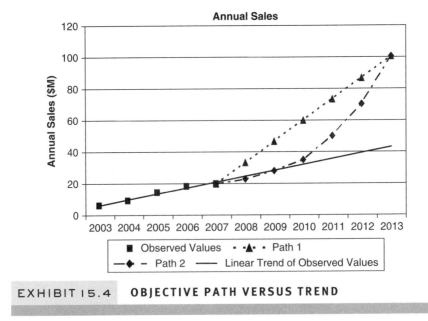

EXHIBIT 15.4   **OBJECTIVE PATH VERSUS TREND**

Publishing the exhibit at the commencement of the objective period would be a great idea as it demonstrates the degree of change achievement of the strategic objective will bring.

It is important for Ms. Objective and Mr. Distribution to agree to the desired path; that is, the one that they will both strive to achieve. It is important for at least two reasons: (1) Mr. Distribution has to be working toward the same objective as Ms. Objective and (2) motivation. I will not go into it too much, but you can imagine that if path 1 was selected as the target path and annual sales reached something less than $33.3 million at the end of 2008, spirits may be dampened. By just looking at the exhibit, you can see that path 2 seems more achievable in 2008 and 2009 than path 1. However, path 2 requires much larger sales *growth* in the final years of the objective period, and this might not sit well with Ms. Objective. Nonetheless, both paths meet the statement of strategic objective: to increase sales over six years to $100 million in 2013. Path 2 seems to me a better choice because it allows you more time to influence the outcomes favorably. Let us assume that Ms. Objective and Mr. Distribution agree to strive to achieve path 2. Our strategic objective is now clear, and we are ready to proceed to set metrics.

EXHIBIT 15.5   **TARGET METRIC VALUES**

Year	Metric Target
2008	23
2009	28
2010	35
2011	50
2012	70
2013	100

Setting metrics includes determining the appropriate metrics and setting target and possibly trigger values for them. To keep the example simple, we will define just one metric per metric class.

The strategic objective metric for this objective seems quite obvious: annual sales. The target value is $100 million in 2013, and we have agreed target values for the interim years. The target values for the interim years are those shown in path 1 (see Exhibit 15.5).

We are done with the strategic objective metric; it will be annual sales. Let us consider the other metric classes. (First let me take one more minute on the strategic objective metric. You could ask whether $100 million should be measured in today's terms or in future terms. Imagine the rather extreme case where inflation is running at 20% annually. Under that case, current sales of $20 million would equate to sales of around $60 million in 2013. Achieving sales of $100 million would equate to real growth of a bit more than 50%. If $100 million really means five times current sales, we would need to achieve sales of around $300 million in 2013. We will continue on the basis that inflation is at normal levels and that it does not make much difference, so $100 million means . . . $100 million.)

Recall the methods we have available for determining risk driver and control indicator metrics: cause-and-effect analysis (and diagrams), why, why, why? analysis, and causal loop diagrams. Given that the organization has five years of sales data available, the analyst should investigate some more sophisticated approaches, such as regression analysis, to determine whether they will be valuable. The analyst should also investigate sales at a more granular level, for example, monthly. It would be unlikely that sales

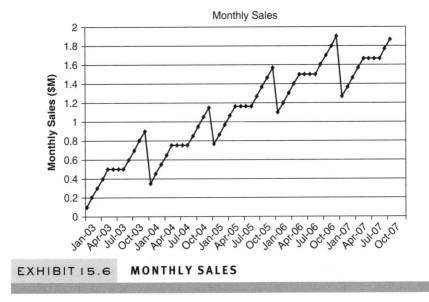

EXHIBIT 15.6   MONTHLY SALES

each month are close to annual sales divided by 12. Let us imagine the organization is involved in business-to-business sales. Such an organization might generate higher sales toward the end of its reporting period and lower sales at the beginning of its reporting period. Analysis of historical sales at this more granular level will be vital if Ms. Objective intends to measure metrics more frequently than annually. From what we have previously discussed, more frequent measurement (though not too frequent) usually is better. Let us just assume the plot of monthly sales looks like Exhibit 15.6.

It is important to understand the historical data in order to forecast the future correctly and interpret observations as they are made. Imagine if you did not analyze monthly sales and observed sales at the end of the first month of the objective period. Without knowing that sales in January are usually the lowest in the year, the January sales data might (or should) cause you to panic. But if you understand how sales behave, you would not panic; your forecast metric values would account for the data.

I digress. Let us get back to determining the other metrics.

In order to determine the risk driver and control metrics, we need to understand what annual sales is and what influences it. Let us say that annual sales is the sum of monthly sales, and monthly sales is the product of units sold and sale price. We can express it mathematically as follows:

$$AS = sum(Jan-Dec)\{units\ sold \times unit\ price\}$$

This formula may not be appropriate in all cases. If not, just modify it. I have used this formula because it lends itself well to what I am going to do next.

Given that annual sales is some function of units sold and unit price, we can immediately determine two factors that influence annual sales: units sold and unit price. We can observe that, assuming other things remain constant:

- An increase in units sold will increase annual sales.
- A decrease in units sold will reduce annual sales.
- An increase in unit price will increase annual sales.
- A decrease in unit price will reduce annual sales.

Without further ado, let us set the number of units sold and unit price as risk driver metrics. Did I say that we would only set one metric? These two came very easily, so we may as well continue with them. We have just performed a cause-and-effect analysis, resulting in the definition of two risk driver metrics. A thorough analysis of the relationship between unit price and units sold is now required, in order to determine price elasticity of demand, but we are going to skip it because this is just an example. Recall, however, that we really want to set metrics that are leading indicators of risk. Although monthly sales are indeed leading indicators of annual sales, we probably can do better than that. We will cover this in a moment when we conduct the formal analysis to determine metrics; right now we are really just throwing around some ideas.

From the graph of monthly sales (Exhibit 15.6), we would be prompted to ask: Why are sales lower at the beginning of the year, flat in the middle, and higher at the end? Let us imagine we find three reasons for the sales pattern:

1. Salespeople generally take leave at the beginning of the year and so the number of man-hours spent "selling" is much lower.
2. Customers generally are very busy in the middle of the year and claim they do not have time to consider purchasing what you sell.

3. Your organization has always offered sales incentives for achieving (monthly) sales in excess of (monthly) quota in the last three months, which leads salespeople to work harder.

Let us immediately define a control metric: number of salesperson days in the month. We will calculate the control metric value this way:

$$CMV = \text{sum(number of salespeople)}\{\text{days at work}\}$$

It would be possible and useful to set a trigger value for this control metric that serves to warn you when the number of salesperson days is too low. The trigger value for this metric would be determined by examining the historical data (in particular, the data from the first few months of the year where the effect of fewer salesperson days is apparent).

So without really trying, we have set at least one metric per objective class. That is great, but the SOAR methodology is based on applying discipline, and I am supposed to be providing an example of the application of the SOAR process, so I had better do it properly. We will take a quick look at the application of each of the approaches mentioned earlier, noting that some are more appropriate than others.

Cause and Effect (and Why, Why, Why?)

We have pretty much covered cause and effect in our rambling. Let me just go through what we did. The first thing we did is ask: What is *annual sales*? We decided to think of annual sales as the sum of monthly sales. Monthly sales is, of course, the sum of daily sales, and daily sales are the sum of minute-by-minute sales. In a retail organization, you probably can enjoy the ability to monitor minute-by-minute sales. Because we are using a business-to-business organization for this example, I have taken the view that monthly would be an appropriate frequency of observation. It means that for each target level of annual sales (of which there are six), we have 12 leading indicators. We also observed that the sales figure is the product of units sold and unit price. We are still defining (annual) sales at this point—we have not started the cause-and-effect analysis just yet. Having recognized sales as the product of units sold and unit price, we are ready to proceed to the cause-and-effect analysis.

Expressed mathematically, we have:

$$\text{Sales} = \text{units sold} \times \text{unit price}$$

It is clear that units sold and unit price are causes of sales. We proceed to set these metrics:

- Units sold is a risk driver metric. It is the count of units sold during the calendar month, and it is observed monthly.

- Unit price is a risk driver metric. It is the average unit price of units sold during the month, and it is observed monthly.

If the organization sells a range of products, it would be sensible to define the metrics at the product level. Even if you sell thousands of units of thousands of products per day, collection of the data should not be an issue. The data is probably collected for some other purpose—reordering, for example.

Now we want to go behind units sold and unit price. So, applying the why, why, why? concept, we ask: Why does units sold behave as it does? (For now, assume that our historical data shows a stable unit price, so the variation in sales is entirely due to variation in units sold.) Again, we have answered it a little earlier; units sold is directly related to the number of salesperson days. So we ask: Why do so many salespeople take leave at the beginning of the year? and we learn that they are required to! Each year, the organization requires that salespeople take a minimum of two weeks annual leave during January or February. This leads us to ask: Why do we demand that salespeople take leave in January or February? and we learn that the organization believes that buyers are not ready to buy so early in the year. We check the complete history of sales and annual leave data, and we observe that the leave policy has always been in force and adhered to. For this reason, we cannot tell, from our data, whether having more salespeople at work during January or February would generate more sales. We note that down as something to investigate further. We proceed to set another metric:

- Salesperson days is a control metric. It is the *forecast* number of salesperson days in the next month, taking approved leave into consideration.

Defining this as a leading indicator gives the organization the opportunity to change it.

We have also been told that units sold flattens over May to August, when buyers do not have time for us because they are busy with other things. We could ask: Why do they need so much time to decide to buy our product? or Why do we have to sell to those people who are busy within our customer organization? Recognizing that some things are beyond our control, we accept the answers:

1. Because our product is very sophisticated and costs a reasonable amount of money, so customers perform extensive analysis and testing of our product as well as that of our competitors as part of their buying process.

2. The decision to purchase our product is almost always made by a buying committee comprised of senior management of the organization, and these same people are involved in preparation of financial statements and annual general meetings during this period.

Now let us examine the last few months of the year. We are told that the organization offers incentives based on overachievement of monthly quotas and that this causes a lift in sales activity and sales. This prompts a couple of why? questions, such as:

- If the incentives lead to an increase in sales activity and this leads to an increase in sales, why do we not offer the incentives every month?

- If we have observed that an increase in sales activity leads to an increase in sales, why do we not hire more salespeople?

If you consider the answers to those questions for a minute, you will see that the role of the enterprise risk manager includes investigating all parts of the organization. The impact of offering incentives probably will need to be considered by the finance department, for example. It is natural for the head of sales to want to offer more incentives, just as it is natural for the head of finance to want to offer fewer, as they represent a reduction in profit. It is understandable that the head of sales may not want to spend time discussing it with the head of finance. It is understandable that neither department head wants to take time to properly analyze the relationships among incentives, sales, and profit. Enter the enterprise risk manager! We could set another control metric here that relates to the level of incentive offered, but in the interest of keeping it simple, we will not.

Cause-and-Effect Diagrams

In this case, I do not think it is necessary to draw a cause-and-effect diagram. These diagrams become most useful when you have multiple objectives with common influential factors (i.e., risk driver or control metrics).

Causal Loop Diagrams

As far as the enterprise risk manager is concerned, causal loop diagrams provide the same information as cause-and-effect diagrams. I have put them both in this book only because I have observed that many people think they are different, although I am not sure why. In our simple example, we do not need a diagram that depicts causes and effects, regardless of what it is called.

Process Flowcharts

At this point, I am not completely happy with the risk driver metrics we have defined. Although they relate to monthly sales and monthly sales is a leading indicator of annual sales, I would prefer to have set one or two metrics that represent leading indicators of monthly sales. A process flow chart (or diagram) of the sales process might help us. Imagine the sales process comprises these steps:

Step	Duration (days)
Introduction	1
Initial promotion of product	2
Proceed/do not proceed	0
Active promotion of product	5
Customer due diligence	20
Proceed/do not proceed	0
Contract negotiation	5
Purchase	0

In this summary of the sales process, the duration has been calculated as the average time taken to perform this step in historical sales. The summary shows that the purchase occurs (on average) 33 days or about 1.5 working months after the first introduction. Great; now we can start to forecast units sold. What else do we need to forecast units sold? Well, we need some idea of our success rate. Again, we can obtain this by observing our historical success rate. Let us say we have a success rate of 25% (i.e., based on our historical sales data, we make one sale for every four introductions). We can now define another risk driver metric. The metric will be:

The number of introductions made, observed on a monthly basis

Regression Analysis

The value of regression analysis is best determined in the presence of the available data. For high-volume variables, such as retail sales, regression usually proves fruitful in uncovering the factors that influence the outcome. In our example, regression analysis is not possible because I have not constructed any data to support it.

Sensitivity Analysis

Sensitivity analysis can be applied when you have some sort of model that describes your strategic objective metric in terms of other things. It can be used to determine the relative importance of those other things (i.e., the impact one thing has on the strategic objective relative to the impact some other thing has on the strategic objective metric). The one thing and the other thing are likely things that you should consider setting as metrics. I guess it is not really the sensitivity analysis that helps you set the metrics; it is the model that describes the strategic objective metric in terms of other things. You really use sensitivity analysis to help you determine the relative importance of the risk driver/control metrics. If risk driver X has 10 times more influence on the strategic objective metric than metric Y, focus on X. From our earlier rambling, we can imagine that sales are a function of (among other things) salesperson-hours.

Scenario Analysis

Scenario analysis is where experts sit down to determine what might happen and what the consequence would be. Their work can be valuable in helping us identify risk driver and control metrics and by enriching our understanding of the probability distribution of metric values. Imagine that the experts believe that there is a 1% probability that 20% of the sales force will come down with the flu, and this will reduce sales by 15%. From this scenario description, we can set a control metric: the percentage of salespeople who have received a flu vaccination. We can also add a point to our distribution.

The outputs of the set step are the metrics. They are summarized in Exhibit 15.7.

Some entries under "Target Value" and "Trigger Value" in Exhibit 15.7 need further explanation:

- 100 is the ultimate target value. We also define target values for each of the five other years.

- X and Y are some numbers that we define for each month within the objective period.

- The sum of the products of X and Y for each 12-month period need to equal the target values of the strategic objective metric.

EXHIBIT 15.7   METRICS DETERMINED BY SCENARIO ANALYSIS

Metric	Metric Class	Measurement	Target Value	Trigger Value
Annual sales	Strategic objective	Annual sales in U.S. dollars	100	n/a
Units sold	Risk driver	Count of units sold in a month	X	n/a
Unit price	Risk driver	Average unit price of units sold in the month	Y	n/a
Salesperson days	Control	Count of salesperson days	Z	T
Introductions	Control	Count of introductions made in the month	4 times X	I

- Z and T are defined by analysis of the historical relationship between salesperson days and sales.
- We set the target value for the metric "Introductions" at four times X because we have historically enjoyed a 25% conversion rate.

STEP 2. OBSERVE (END-OF-YEAR METRIC VALUES)

For this part, I am obviously going to make up the metric values. We will jump forward to one year from the commencement of the objective period. The metric values for the year are shown in Exhibit 15.8.

Two items on the exhibit need explanation. One is "Monthly Sales." We said that we would observe units sold and sale price; let us pretend we did that, and we noticed that the unit price remained constant over the observation period. In this case, there is little point decomposing monthly sales into number and price, so we will just report sales. (We do lose a little visibility of the direct relationship between the number of introductions

EXHIBIT 15.8   OBSERVED METRIC VALUES

Month	Salesperson Days	Introductions	Monthly Sales ($M)	Annual Sales (YTD $M)
Nov-07		64		
Dec-07		68		
Jan-08	100	72	1.6	1.6
Feb-08	120	76	1.7	3.3
Mar-08	180	105	1.8	5.1
Apr-08	190	110	1.9	7
May-08	170	115	2.1	9.1
Jun-08	170	120	2.2	11.3
Jul-08	175	130	2.3	13.6
Aug-08	180	135	2.4	16
Sep-08	190	120	2.6	18.6
Oct-08	200	115	2.7	21.3
Nov-08	160	110	2.8	24.1
Dec-08	120	100	2.9	27

and the *number* of sales. I am not suggesting we would stop recording the metrics—certainly not; we may just choose to publish them in this slightly different manner.) In the previous example of a SOAR analysis, we described how the volatility in one metric related to the volatility in another. If a metric displays very little volatility, you should question its value as a metric. In this example, when we determined the metric, we did so without examining the history of unit prices. This was, in hindsight, a mistake. Had we analyzed the volatility of historical observations of unit price and seen that unit price was very stable, we would have set the metric at either the count of sales or the dollar value of sales. Mistakes almost always provide very valuable information for later use. In our case, we will apply what we have learned from this mistake the next time we set metrics.

Consider a couple of methods available for setting metrics and you will see that, had we applied them more thoughtfully, they would have led us to the correct conclusion: that unit price need not be a metric. Sensitivity analysis, for example. We sort of applied it, but not completely. We recognized sales (in U.S. dollars) as a function of units sold and unit price. We then just assumed that both of those factors could fluctuate and that the movement in sales (U.S. dollars) would be as a result of the movements in units sold and unit price. Without fluctuation, or variability, or volatility, or whatever you like to call it, a metric can influence another metric but not influence the volatility of that metric.

The other item in the exhibit requiring some explanation is the "Annual Sales" metric value. I know I said that it would be observed annually, because that is the only time it can be observed, but we can record sales year-to-date as we go, so why not do so? By the way, I am guessing that you figured out why the measurement starts from November 2007: because we know the sales cycle takes about six weeks, right?

That is all we need for the observe step—to observe the metric values.

STEP 3. ANALYZE (MOVEMENTS IN METRIC VALUES)

In the interest of time, I will examine just one end-of-year point in the objective period rather than analyzing 6 years of 12 months of completely fictitious data. In a real operation, you would conduct analysis on a monthly basis.

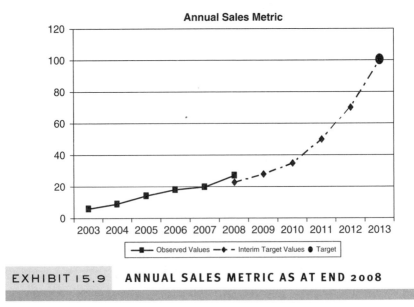

EXHIBIT 15.9   ANNUAL SALES METRIC AS AT END 2008

Let us begin by plotting what we have observed during 2008. First, we will plot the strategic objective metric on its own, as we did in the beginning (see Exhibit 15.9).

You know the response from senior management: "Great, we are ahead of forecast!"

Your response would include repeating that the interim target values represent a single point (e.g., the mean) on a distribution of possible values and that the observed value falls within the forecast range, which could be shown in a number of ways, including the example shown in Exhibit 15.10.

This exhibit shows that the achieved level of annual sales was the maximum forecast level, but it does not reveal the probability we assigned to that value. It could be that our distribution comprised only three points: a value of 19 with a probability of 25%, a value of 23 with a probability of 50%, and a value of 27 with a probability of 25%. More likely, however, is that if the value is the maximum of our distribution, it boasts some very small probability—say around 1%. If I were Mr. Distribution, I would be concerned about the reliability of the forecast, and I would ensure that the analysis fully explained how we managed to achieve what we thought

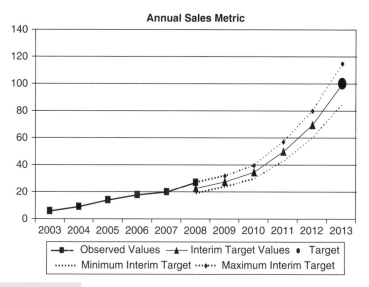

EXHIBIT 15.10   FORECAST ANNUAL SALES METRIC VALUES

to be a very unlikely result, even though it is a good one—because good is as bad as bad.

Let us quickly drop in a trend line for the strategic objective metric, recognizing that we consider the 2008 sales level to be a freak result (due to the fact that we assigned it somewhere around 1% probability) (see Exhibit 15.11).

The exhibit including the trend line is not something I would publish, because it might allow people to relax a little. As enterprise risk managers, we really should, until we have reason to believe otherwise, treat the most recent observation as unlikely. With any luck, the analysis will provide some great explanation for the outcome and the forecast; for example, it will explain that when the forecast was made, the two new salespeople who had been hired but did not start until March were not registered in the human resources system and so we did not include the additional sales days in our forecast. Since this is just an example, let us allow the analysis to reveal that the increase in sales was due to the addition of two new salespeople and that they were not considered in the forecast.

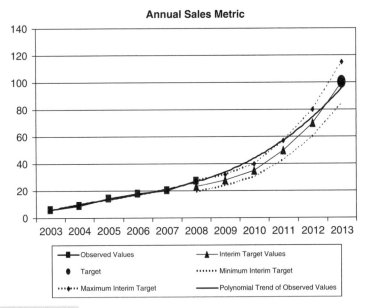

Annual Sales Metric

━■━ Observed Values	━▲━ Interim Target Values
● Target	•••••• Minimum Interim Target
•••◆••• Maximum Interim Target	──── Polynomial Trend of Observed Values

EXHIBIT 15.11   **FORECAST ANNUAL SALES METRIC VALUES WITH TREND**

An examination of observed values of the monthly sales metric reveals a change in the shape of sales. In Exhibit 15.12, we can see the observed values of monthly sales for 2007 and 2008. Recall that sales had followed a distinct pattern: relatively low in the first few months, flat in the middle, and relatively high at the end.

As you might guess, we determine (and note for consideration in future forecasts) that the cause of the uplift from the middle of the year was due to the new business resulting from the addition of two new, enthusiastic sales-people at least six weeks earlier. That becomes slightly more apparent when we plot all the metrics in Exhibit 15.13.

Exhibit 15.13 reveals a very strong correlation between introductions and monthly sales. If we were not aware of the length of the sales cycle (which creates the lagged effect between sales and introductions), we might interpret the deviation in the lines for these metrics in the last two months of the year as a break in the pattern. However, because we are aware of the lagged effect, we imagine a downturn in monthly sales in January and February 2009 in line with the downturn in introductions in November and December 2008.

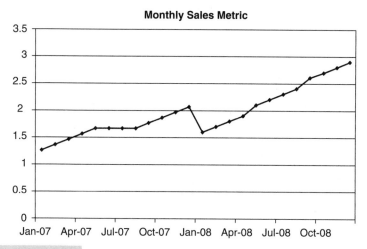

EXHIBIT 15.12   **MONTHLY SALES METRIC**

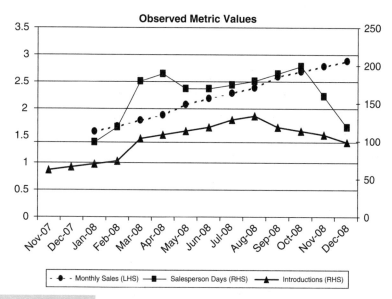

EXHIBIT 15.13   **MONTHLY METRIC OBSERVATIONS**

That is probably as much analysis as we need to perform. The second part of the analyze step is to disseminate the information to interested parties, in particular to the "Ms. Objectives." Exhibit 15.14 is an example of the report we might provide.

EXHIBIT 15.14   EXAMPLE SOAR ANALYSIS REPORT

Date of analysis: January 1, 2009

Summary of Strategic Objective
Strategic objective: to increase annual sales over the period January 1, 2008, to December 31, 2013 to achieve sales of $100 million in 2013

STRATEGIC OBJECTIVE METRIC: ANNUAL SALES IN 2013 (INTERIM TARGET VALUES AS SHOWN)

Year	Metric Target
2008	23
2009	28
2010	35
2011	50
2012	70

Risk driver metric(s):
Monthly sales, measured in U.S. $000,000
Control metric(s):
Salesperson days, measured as the estimated number of salesperson days in the next month
Introductions, measured as the count of introductory meetings held by salespeople during the month

STRATEGIC OBJECTIVE METRIC VALUES (DATA)

Year	Forecast Minimum	Forecast Average	Forecast Maximum	Observed Value
2008	19	23	27	27
2009	24	28	32	
2010	30	35	40	
2011	43	50	57	
2012	60	70	80	
2013	85	100	115	

STRATEGIC OBJECTIVE METRIC VALUES PLOT

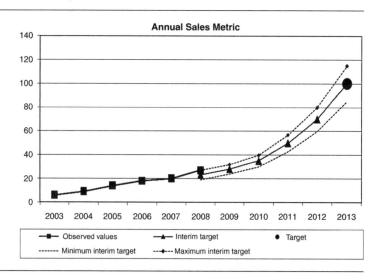

RISK DRIVER AND CONTROL METRIC VALUES PLOT

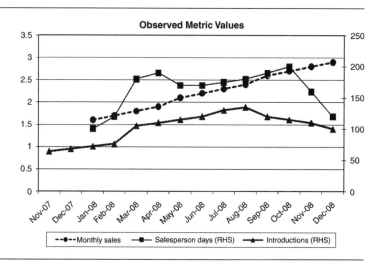

Validation of Observed Metric Values Description
Each number was validated by the Enterprise Risk Management office.

Behavior in Metrics Analysis
The data shows a very strong correlation between the number of introductory meetings held by salespeople and the number (and therefore dollar amount) of sales (two

(Continued)

EXHIBIT 15.14   (CONTINUED)

months later). Sales during 2008 behaved quite differently from the typical behavior observed in the preceding five years. In previous years, sales were low in January, increased over February to May, remained flat over June to August, and then increased each month during September to December. In 2008, sales increased every month, starting around $1.5 million in January and ending around $3 million in December. We have identified the addition of two new salespeople in March as the cause of the increase in sales over the middle of the year. This raises questions about our current belief that potential buyers are too busy to consider purchasing during this period.

Review of Forecast Description
Our previous forecast of monthly (and therefore annual) sales applied the historical trend of flat sales in the middle of the year and did not take into consideration the addition of two salespeople. Recognizing the high correlation between introductions and sales, and the strong relationship between salesperson days and introductions, our reviewed forecast appears next. The minimum values are based on the notion that the sales achieved by the two new salespeople were a result of their enthusiasm and that this may not continue. The maximum values are based on the notion that sales growth can be achieved during the middle months of the year. In addition, minimum values are based on an assumption of fewer salesperson days, based on sickness and departure of salespeople. Maximum values assume a low level of absenteeism and no departures. We provide a forecast of metric values for each month of 2009 and a forecast of the interim and ultimate strategic objective metric values for the remaining objective period. The forecast for 2009 includes the observed values of introductions for the last two months of 2008, as we know that introductions are a leading indicator of sales. The forecast for the remainder of the objective period includes observed values of the metric prior to commencement of the objective as a basis for the trend line. A key assumption behind our forecast for the strategic objective metric is an increase in the number of salespeople, by one at the end of 2010 and another at the end of 2011.

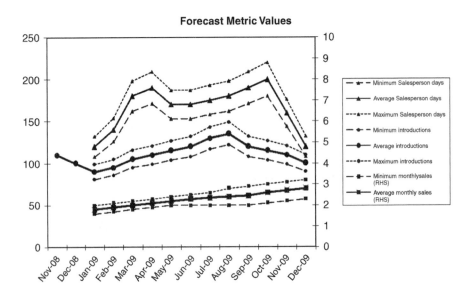

Forecast Metric Values

Strategic Objective Metric (Annual Sales)

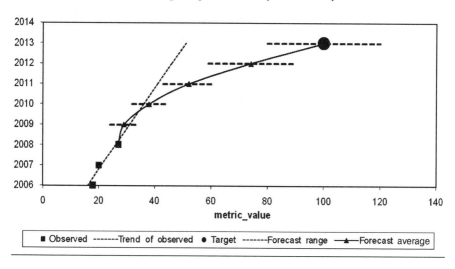

Legend: ■ Observed -------Trend of observed ● Target -------Forecast range —▲—Forecast average

STEP 4. REACT (TO THE END-OF-YEAR ANALYSIS)

I am going to put myself in the shoes of Ms. Objective for a moment. As Ms. Objective, I think my reaction would be something like "Are you nuts? There is no way we can achieve that rate of growth!" Mr. Distribution should sit Ms. Objective down and explain the basis of the forecast, in particular pointing out a couple of the basic facts revealed by the analysis:

- There is a reasonably high correlation between salesperson days and introductions.
- There is a very high correlation between introductions and sales.
- It has been proven that customers *can* buy in what were previously thought to be too-busy-to-buy months.

Now that Ms. Objective understands this, you would hope her reaction might be something like this: "So you're saying that if we have more people making more introductory calls, we can achieve this objective?" Mr. Distribution might respond: "I'm just telling you what the data suggests." Let us not forget that we did not produce the report in order to get an interesting reaction from Ms. Objective. We distribute the reports to provide the objective owners the data they need to make decisions and take actions appropriate to what the analysis reveals. Our analysis clearly states that there is a strong relationship between sales activity (i.e., introductions and sales-person days bundled together) and sales. The reaction from the objective owner should be obvious: increase the level of sales activity. If he or she does that, we should see the positive effect when we next observe the metrics (subject to lead time, of course). If the analysis stimulates an appropriate reaction and the impact of that reaction is evident in a subsequent observation and analysis period, the enterprise risk manager has served the organization well.

Step 1. Set

If you are wondering why we are back at the set step, review the SOAR process flow diagram again (see Exhibit 15.15).

We have come back to step 1 to demonstrate and remind you that the entire process is iterative. Sometimes the analysis may lead you to the conclusion that you are not tracking the right metrics. In such a case, you will have to set new metrics. In our example, we can take comfort in the strong relationships we see between our risk driver and strategic objective metrics and our control and risk driver metrics. If you are wondering about these "strong relationships," take another look at how we defined the risk elements (see Exhibit 15.16).

You see how we sometimes attach controls to risk drivers? Because we have defined the number of sales as the risk driver and introductions as a control, we need to check whether that relationship remains, which indeed it does.

Step 2. Observe

There is no need for me to create some data to put here, I am sure. The purpose of the repetition is to reinforce that the process is repetitive. There is something else that I hope, by now, you have found repetitive, and that is the presentation of data in the form of a graph. Take a moment to fan the pages of this book and see how many graphs there are. I'll explain why in the next section.

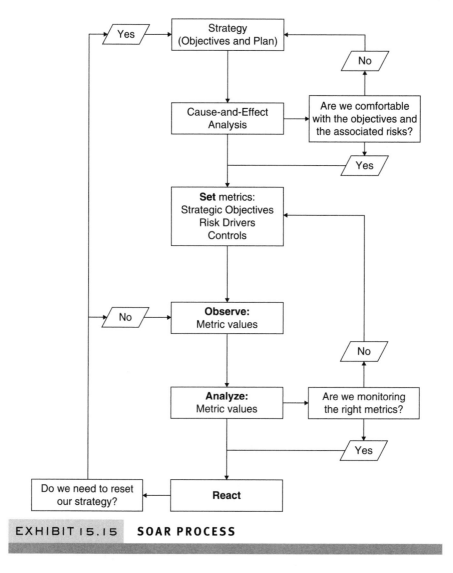

EXHIBIT 15.15   SOAR PROCESS

Step 3. Analyze

Because we are not going to analyze a second set of fictitious data, I will take the opportunity to discuss two things: (1) why I think the presentation of data in the form of graphs is important, and (2) the analysis we performed at the end of 2008.

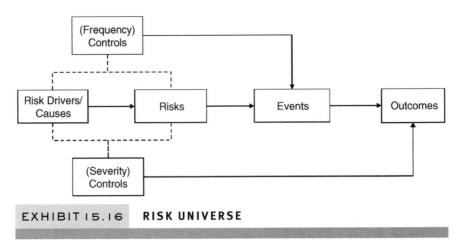

EXHIBIT 15.16   RISK UNIVERSE

Let me explain why I think graphs are important. First and foremost, the probability distribution is the foundation of the SOAR methodology, and the probability distribution can be understood very easily when it is presented graphically. I hope that, having reached this point, you will agree. Second, I believe that some things are hard to see in tabulated data but are quite clear on a graph. Having said that, I think it is possible—in fact, some people make it look very easy—to produce very awkward graphs. Exhibit 15.17 is a copy of one of the graphs that appeared in the example analysis; the only difference is a change to the right-hand scale.

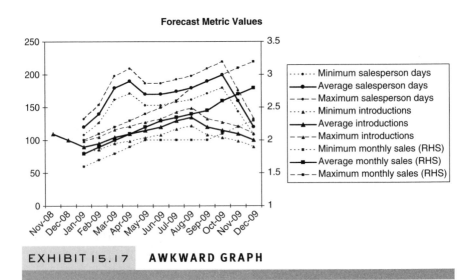

EXHIBIT 15.17   AWKWARD GRAPH

Obviously I'm exaggerating by making such a miserable graph; my point is that when you produce a graph, take a moment to check whether the graph alone tells the story you want it to.

Now I would like to make one observation on the analysis we conducted earlier. Some of you may have picked up on the fact that the range of forecast values for the strategic objective metric at the end of 2013 was wider in our 2008 analysis than at the beginning of the objective period. First, let me congratulate those of you who noticed this; you really are paying attention to detail. Those of you who did not should not feel disappointed. I previously stated that the role of the enterprise risk manager is to help the organization create a set of circumstances that leads to a taller, thinner distribution of possible outcomes associated with the strategic objective. That the range of forecast values became wider means the probability distribution certainly became wider; it may also have become shorter. It happened because the enterprise risk management office took a conservative view in regard to the change in sales pattern in 2008. Although we have been able to confirm that the lift in sales during the traditionally flat period was due to the arrival of new salespeople, we can not be sure whether the lift is repeatable. It could be, for example, that buyers are very busy during those months and push salespeople away as much as possible and that the two new salespeople managed to make sales because they were so aggressive. We do not know what the objective owner will do in this case. We could, for example, offer to do further analysis, which might include interviewing the new salespeople to find out how they made those sales and then compare their approaches to those of less successful salespeople. We could do that, but shouldn't the head of sales, the strategic objective owner, do that? I think he or she should. But if that person does not, we should. Someone has to, because that is what the process is all about.

Step 4. React

Enterprise risk management officers should do all that they can to control the objective owner's reaction. By that I mean they should provide enough information about the historical data they have studied and the forecasts they have made to clarify what factors positively and negatively impact the objective owner's chance of achieving the strategic objective. In a way, enterprise risk management officers should be able to make things happen.

For example, in the earlier analysis, I noted that one assumption related to the employment of two additional salespeople: one in 2010 and the second in 2011. In this way, we have turned the forecast into a sort of resource planning tool. Rather than say "Well, we've got 10 salespeople, so we expect to reach sales of between $60 and $80 million," we say "In order to reach $100 million, we need to hire two new salespeople." Then the organization is armed with the data it needs to make resource allocation decisions. If the strategic objective is important to the organization, it will hire new people. If it is not important, fine; stop wasting resources applying the SOAR methodology to something that is not significant.

Conclusion

Thank you for reading this book, which has launched the SOAR methodology, at the heart of which is the SOAR process. When used in the phrase "the SOAR methodology," SOAR is an acronym for strategic objectives at risk. When used in the phrase "the SOAR process," SOAR is an acronym for the four steps of the process: set, observe, analyze, and react.

Key to successful application of the SOAR methodology is a basic understanding of and a great appreciation of the probability distribution. Accordingly, a significant amount of this book has been devoted to discussing probability distributions, albeit at a very unsophisticated level. The central philosophy of the SOAR methodology is that a number of not equally desirable outcomes are possible as objective owners strive to achieve the strategic objectives assigned to them. The SOAR process is a disciplined approach to analyzing, understanding, and influencing the probabilities of the various outcomes. The primary objective of the enterprise risk management office, responsible for the management and execution of the SOAR process, is to help objective owners act to reduce the probability of undesirable outcomes and increase the probability of desired outcomes. In other words, the primary objective is to help the organization create a set of circumstances that has a taller, thinner distribution of possible outcomes associated with it.

Finally, I would like to invite you to participate in the SOAR methodology. You now know what resources are required, how to run the SOAR process and the benefits you will enjoy. A sequel to this book will include case studies of organizations that have achieved strategic objectives by operating their enterprise risk management office under the SOAR methodology. I invite anyone who applies the SOAR methodology to inform me of their success, by writing to gmonahan@soar-advisory.com.

Before I go, I would like to wish you the best of luck in your endeavour to reach your strategic objectives, because I recognize that luck almost always plays some role.

I wish to leave you with this graph of two probability distributions of possible outcomes:

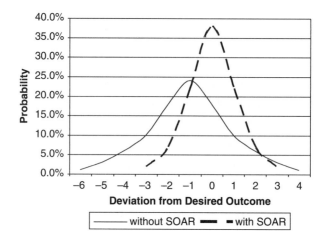

SOAR Methodology FAQ

Typical questions relating to the SOAR methodology and the types of answers a conversant enterprise risk manager should provide follow.

Question 1: What does "SOAR" stand for when used in the phrase "SOAR methodology"?

Answer: Strategic objectives at risk.

Question 2: What does "SOAR" stand for when used in the phrase "SOAR process"?

Answer: Set, observe, analyze, and react.

Question 3: What does a probability distribution of outcomes show?

Answer: The probability distribution of outcomes plots possible outcomes and their associated probabilities.

Question 4: Comment on Exhibit A.1, which shows the probability of outcomes associated with a strategic objective.

Answer: The probability distribution shows that the probability of a very bad outcome (40%) is far greater than the probability of a perfect outcome (just 10%). It shows that the possibility of a bad outcome is relatively high (20%) and the probability of a tolerable outcome is 30%. If we describe tolerable and perfect outcomes as "acceptable" outcomes and everything else as "unacceptable," the probability of unacceptable outcomes is 60%. The distribution could be redrawn as shown in Exhibit A.2.

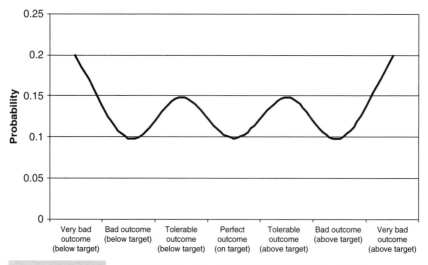

EXHIBIT A.1   **AWKWARD PROBABILITY DISTRIBUTION OF POSSIBLE OUTCOMES**

The distribution of possible outcomes shows that the likelihood of achieving the strategic objective is low relative to the likelihood of a bad or very bad outcome.

Question 5: What is "residual risk"?

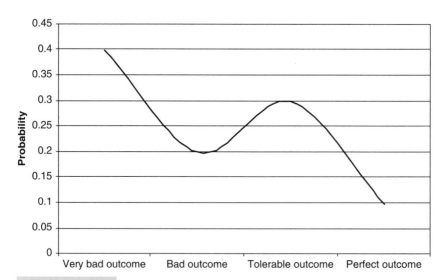

EXHIBIT A.2   **REDISTRIBUTION OF POSSIBLE OUTCOMES**

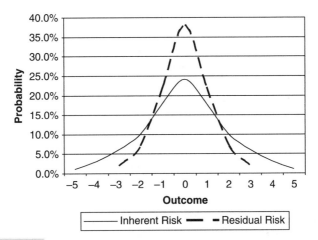

Inherent Risk ▬ ▬ Residual Risk

EXHIBIT A.3   **INHERENT VERSUS RESIDUAL RISK PROBABILITY DISTRIBUTIONS**

Answer: "Residual risk" is the risk that remains after the distribution of possible outcomes has been adjusted to account for the impact of controls. Controls are measures we put in place to influence outcomes, in particular, to reduce the frequency and/or severity of an adverse outcome. The risk that exists prior to the application of controls is referred to as inherent risk. Residual risk can be expressed mathematically as inherent risk minus controls.

Question 6: In Exhibit A.3, which line do you believe represents inherent risk and which represents residual risk? Why?

Answer: Residual risk is the risk that remains after controls have been applied to the inherent risk. The result should be a distribution of possible outcomes that is taller and thinner than the original distribution. The taller line represents residual risk as it is taller and thinner than the shorter line, which represents inherent risk.

Question 7: From Exhibit A.4, what metric value would you forecast for the next period?

Answer: The metric value displays a constant rate of change over the last eight periods, so I have no basis for believing that the value in period 9 would be anything other than 9. I forecast the value of the metric to be 9 in the next period.

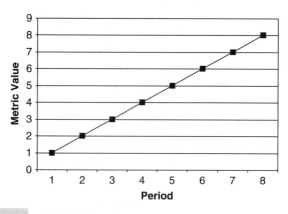

EXHIBIT A.4   LINEAR OBSERVED VALUES

Question 8: From Exhibit A.5, what metric value would you forecast for the next period?

Answer: The metric displays reasonable volatility over the observation period, so I will forecast a range of values. From the observed values, we see that the historical movements have been −50%, +67%, 0, and +2/5. Applying historical simulation, we would estimate these values and probabilities for the next period:

(Note: There are other appropriate answers to this question. A correct answer is one that includes the estimation of a range of possible outcomes and assigns probabilities to them.)

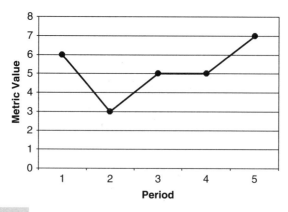

EXHIBIT A.5   NONLINEAR OBSERVED VALUES

Value	Probability
$7 - 50\% \times 7 = 3.5$	25%
$7 + 67\% \times 7 = 11.7$	25%
$7 + 0 \times 7 = 7$	25%
$7 + 2/5 \times 7 = 9.8$	25%

Question 9: Describe the set step of the SOAR process.

Answer: Within the set step, we set metrics. We strive to set one strategic objective metric and at least one metric for each of the remaining metric classes: risk driver metrics and control metrics. The methods available for setting metrics include cause-and-effect analysis, why, why, why? analysis, examination of causal loop and process flow diagrams, regression analysis, sensitivity analysis, and scenario analysis. After setting the metrics, we set a target value for the strategic objective metric and, if useful, trigger values for the other metrics. The movement in the strategic objective metric should be described by the movements in the other metrics.

Question 10: Describe the observe step of the SOAR process.

Answer: The observe step is where we observe metric values at regular intervals. Methods available for observing metric values include gathering available data, calculating data, and self-assessment. We should observe the metric frequently enough to capture material movements in the metric value but not too often.

Question 11: Describe the analyze step of the SOAR process.

Answer: The analyze step is where we analyze the observed metric values. The purpose of the analyze step is twofold: (1) to explain the movements in the metrics with a view to forecasting their future values, and (2) to report the findings of the analysis to stimulate reaction. In the analyze step, we validate data and the choice of metrics. Validation of the choice of metrics includes examination of the correlation between the risk driver and control metrics and the strategic objective metric.

Question 12: Describe the react step of the SOAR process.

Answer: The react step of the SOAR process is triggered by the distribution of reports produced in the analyze step. The react step involves the owner of the strategic objective reacting to the information contained in the analysis. Responsibility for reacting lies with the objective owner, who should record the rationale for his or her reaction so that this data can be available for future analysis.

Resources

Barr, S. "202 Tips for Performance Measurement," 2006, http://www.staceybarr.com/.

Basel Committee on Banking Supervision, Bank for International Settlements, "Sound Practices for the Management and Supervision of Operational Risk," 2005.

Berle, A, and G. Means. *The Modern Corporation and Private Property*. Macmillan, 1932.

Bernstein, P. L. *Against the Gods*. Wiley & Sons, 1996.

Dahl, A L, "Measuring the Unmeasurable," *Our Planet* 8, no.1 (June 1996), www.ourplanet.com/imgversn/81/lyon.html.

Governance Metrics International. "GMI Research Categories and Sample Metrics," http://www. gmiratings.com.

Gupta, P. *Six Sigma Business Scorecard*. McGraw-Hill, 2004.

J. P. Morgan/Reuters, "RiskMetrics—Technical Document," 4th ed. Morgan Guaranty Trust Company of New York, 1996.

Jordan, E, and L. Silcock. *Beating IT Risks*. John Wiley & Sons, 2005.

Kahneman, D., and A. Tversky. "Prospect Theory: An Analysis of Decision under Risk," *Econometrica* 47 (March 1979): 263–291.

Kaplan, R. S., and D. P. Norton. "The Balanced Scorecard—Measures that Drive Performance," *Harvard Business Review* (January–February 1992): 71–79.

Kaplan, R. S., and D. P. Norton. *The Balanced Scorecard: Translating Strategy into Action*. Harvard Business School Press, 1996.

Kaplan, R. S., and D. P. Norton. *Strategy Maps*. Harvard Business School Press, 2004.

Korsan, R. J. *Nothing Ventured, Nothing Gained: Modeling Venture Capital Decisions*. Miller Freeman Publications, 1994.

Kun, M. L. "A Strategy for Achieving Enterprise Risk Management." Gartner Research, 2003.

Magretta, J. *Managing in the New Economy*. Harvard Business Review Books, 1999.

Mintzberg, H., and J. Lampel. "Reflecting on the Strategy Process" in M. Cusumano and C. Markides, eds., *Strategic Thinking for the Next Economy*. Jossey-Bass, 2001.

Modigliani, F., and M. Miller. "The Cost of Capital, Corporate Finance and the Theory of Investment," *American Economic Review* 48 (1958): 48, 261–297.

Moody's Investors Service, "Guide to Moody's Ratings, Rating Process and Rating Practices," 2004.

"Psychological Measurements: Their Uses and Misuses," http://www.uq.edu.au/~mlpjewel/psych_test_misuses.pdf.

RiskMetrics Group. "Risk Management—A Practical Guide," 1999.

Schroder, D. "Investment under Ambiguity with the Best and Worst in Mind," 2006, http://realoptions.org/papers2006/Schroeder_Knight.pdf.

Standard & Poor's. "Corporate Ratings Criteria." 2005.

Standards Australia Limited and Standards New Zealand. "Risk Management—AS/NZS 4360:2004," Joint Technical Committee OB-007 Risk Management, 2004.

Index